Google Nexus 7 Survival Guide

By Toly K

Table of Contents

Getting Started

Table of Contents

1. Button Layout

The Nexus 7 has two buttons and two jacks. With the exception of turning the device on and off and adjusting the volume, the touchscreen is used to control all functions on the device. The device has the following buttons and jacks:

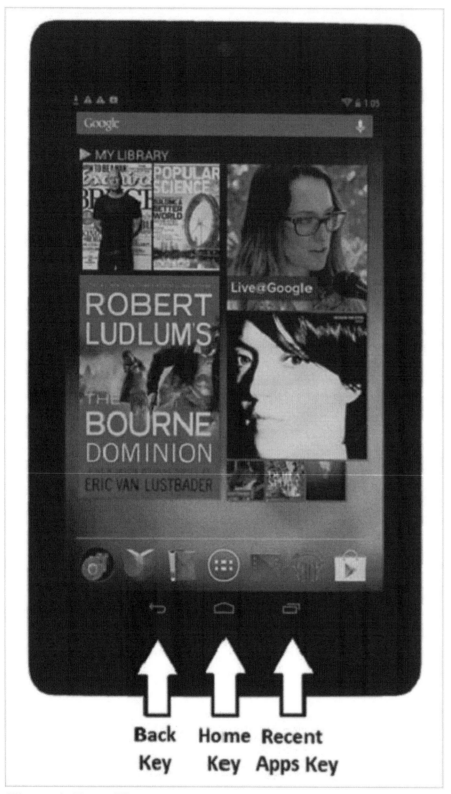

Figure 1: Front View

On-Screen Navigation Keys - The navigation keys described below respond to your touch, so they do not need to be pressed. Touch each key on the screen to perform the corresponding action, as follows:

 - Displays the Home screen at any time.

 - Returns to the previous screen.

 - Shows all recently opened applications.

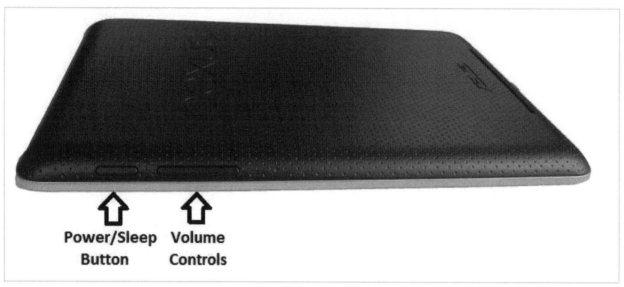

Figure 2: Right Side View

Power/Sleep Button - Turns the Nexus 7 on and off. Pressing it also puts the device to sleep.

Volume Controls - Increases and decreases the media volume.

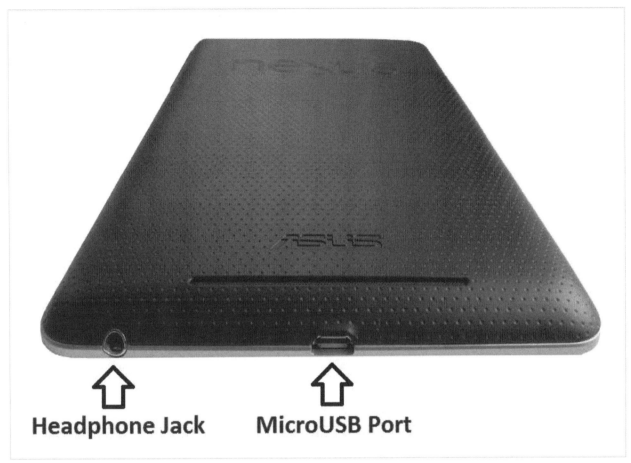

Figure 3: Bottom View

MicroUSB Port - Connects the Nexus 7 to a computer in order to transfer data.

Headphone Jack - Allows headphones to be connected.

2. Charging the Nexus 7

Before using the Nexus 7 for the first time, it is recommended to charge it fully. Using the included charging adapter, plug the Nexus 7 into a power outlet. Do not use a USB port on a computer, as it may not charge the tablet fully. When the Nexus 7 is done charging, the charge percentage is 100%. To charge the Nexus 7 while it is turned off, simply plug it in. The device will not turn itself on when it is plugged in to a power source.

3. Turning the Nexus 7 On and Off

To turn the Nexus 7 on, press and hold the **Power** button for three seconds or until 'Google' appears. The Nexus 7 takes several moments to start up. The first time you turn on the tablet, the Welcome screen appears. Refer to *"Performing First-Time Setup"* on page 16 to learn how to set up your new Nexus 7.

To turn the Nexus 7 off, press and hold the **Power** button until the Power Off window appears, as shown in **Figure 4**. Touch **Power off**. A confirmation dialog appears. Touch **OK**. The Nexus 7 turns off.

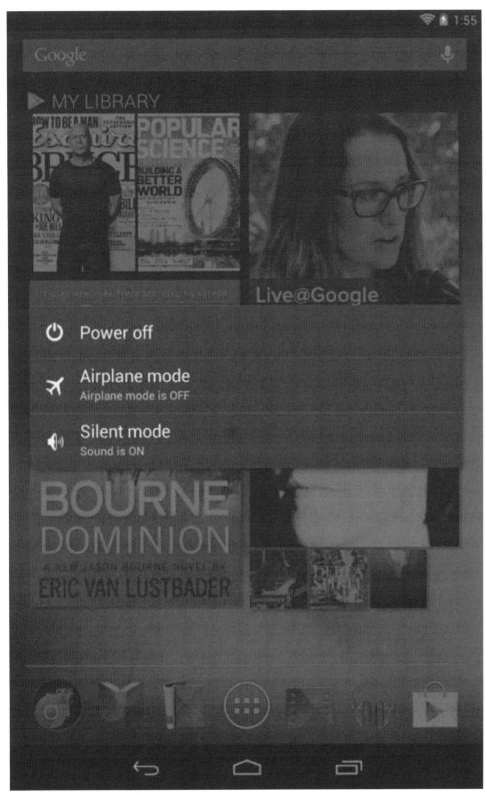

Figure 4: Power Off Window

4. Performing First-Time Setup

When you turn on the Nexus 7 for the first time, you must set it up before you can use it. To perform first-time setup:

1. Turn on the tablet. Refer to *"Turning the Nexus 7 On and Off"* on page 14 to learn how. The Welcome screen appears, as shown in **Figure 5**.

2. Touch the ▶ button. The Wi-Fi Setup screen appears, as shown in **Figure 6**.
3. Touch the network to which you wish to connect. The Network Password prompt appears, as shown in **Figure 7**.
4. Enter your network password (usually found on your wireless router) and touch **Connect**. The Nexus 7 connects to the selected network, provided that the password is correct, and the Sign In screen appears, as shown in **Figure 8**. If you purchased the Nexus 7 from the Play Store, your Gmail address is entered automatically. Otherwise, you will need to enter your Gmail address before proceeding. If you do not have a Google account, use your computer to navigate to **https://accounts.google.com/SignUp** to create one.

5. Enter your Gmail password and touch the ▶ button in the lower right-hand corner of the screen. The Backup and Restore screen appears, as shown in **Figure 9**. By default, both Backup options are enabled.
6. Touch **Restore from my Google Account to this tablet** or **Keep this tablet backed up with my Google Account** to disable either feature. The selected feature is disabled. Touch either option again to re-enable the feature.

7. Touch the ▶ button in the lower right-hand corner of the screen. The Google Location screen appears, as shown in **Figure 10**. By default, both location options are enabled.
8. Touch either option on this screen to disable the corresponding feature. The selected feature are disabled. Touch either option again to re-enable the feature.

9. Touch the ▶ button in the lower right-hand corner of the screen. The Setup Confirmation screen appears.

10. Touch the ▶ button. Your Nexus 7 is setup and ready to use.

donadams 375. DA   Back up email
P. kephalonia   @gmail.com   address
                               dja375@tiscali.co.uk

Figure 5: Welcome Screen

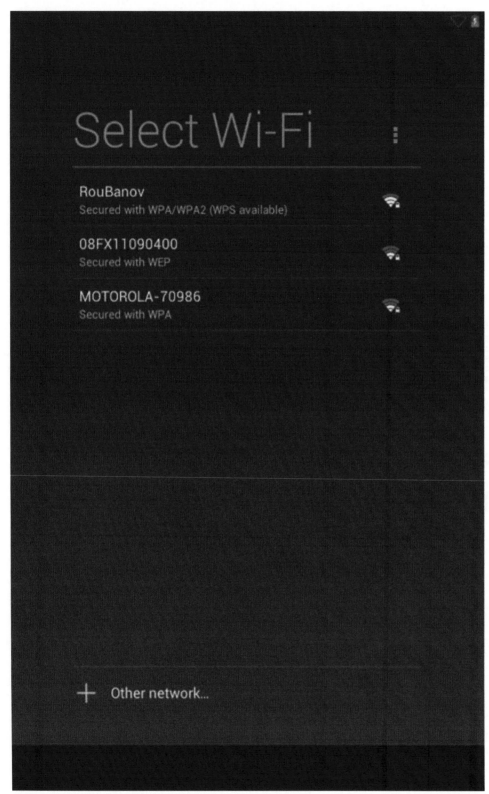

Figure 6: Wi-Fi Setup Screen

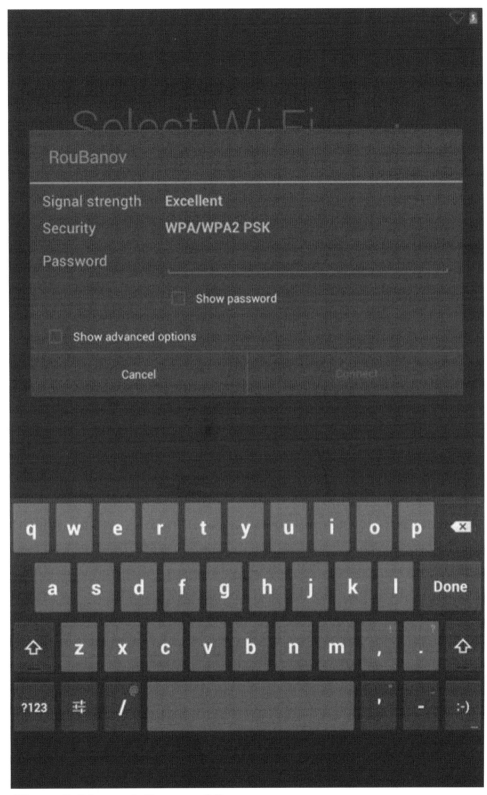

Figure 7: Network Password Prompt

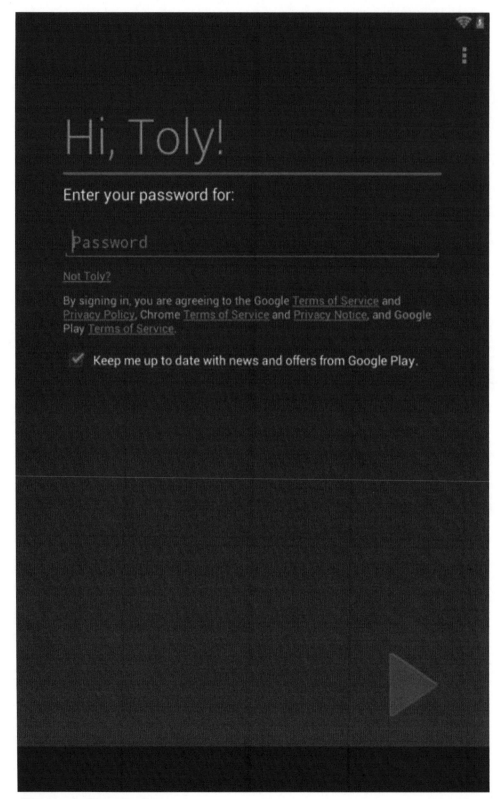

Figure 8: Sign In Screen

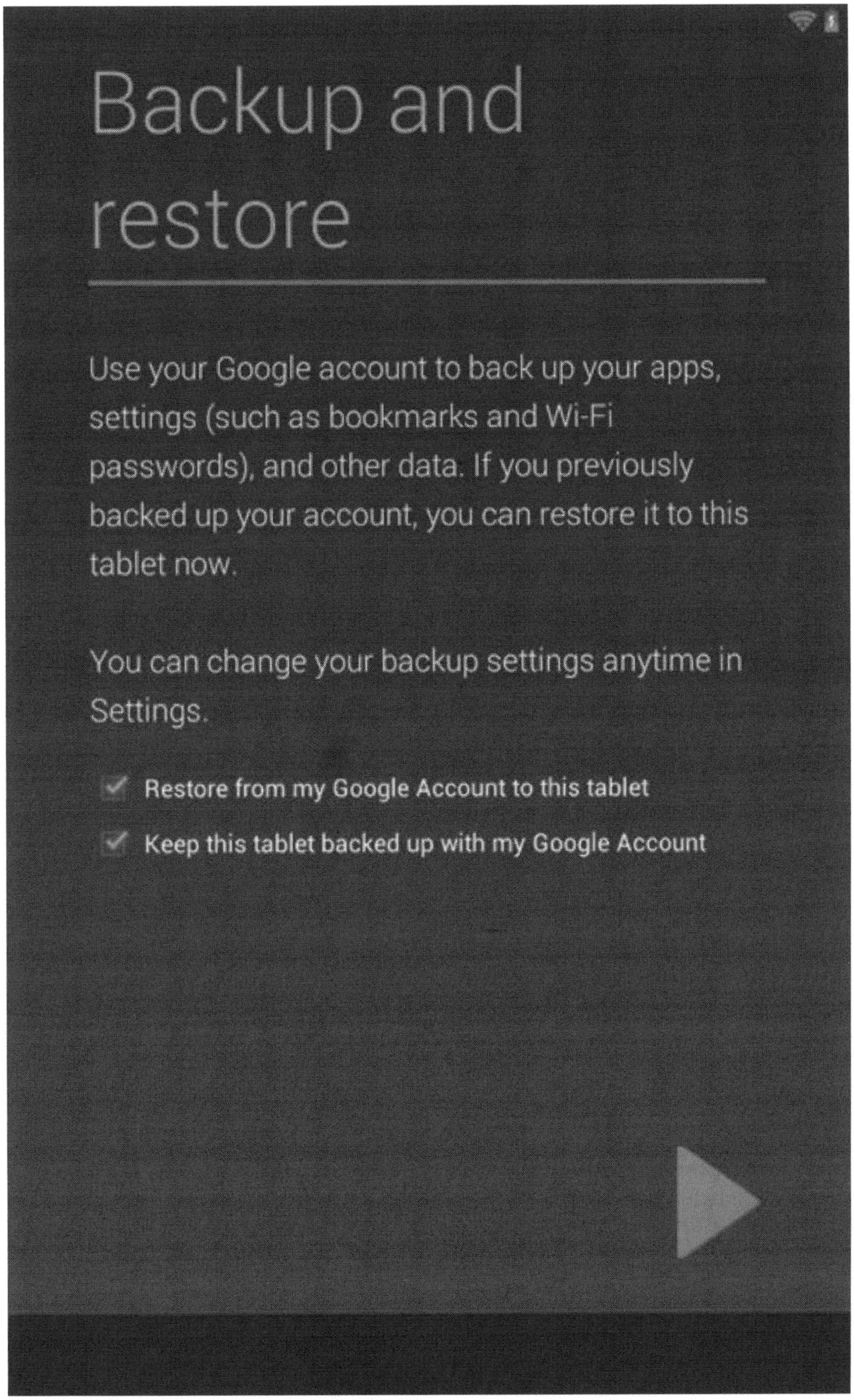

Figure 9: Backup and Restore Screen

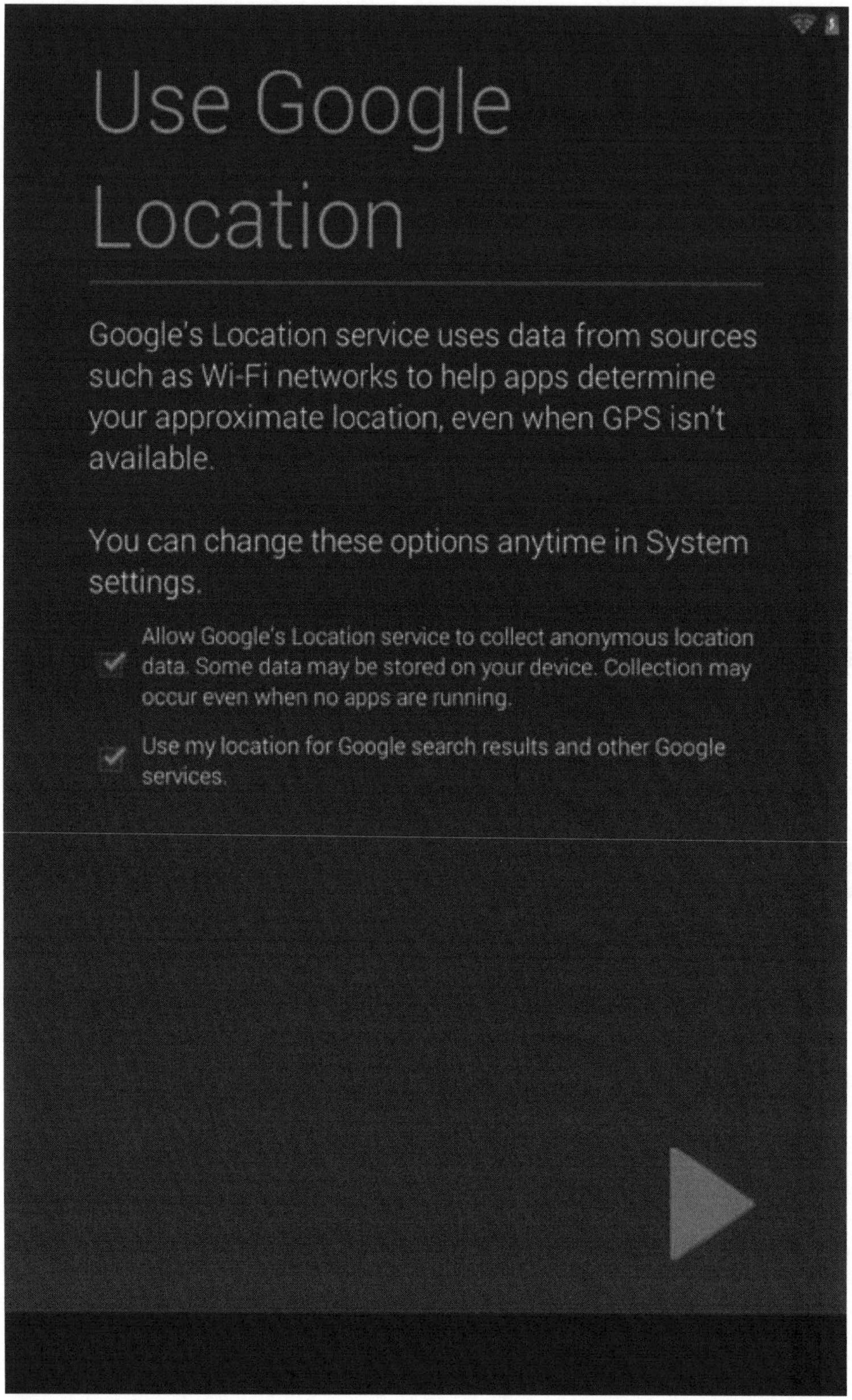

Use Google Location

Google's Location service uses data from sources such as Wi-Fi networks to help apps determine your approximate location, even when GPS isn't available.

You can change these options anytime in System settings.

✓ Allow Google's Location service to collect anonymous location data. Some data may be stored on your device. Collection may occur even when no apps are running.

✓ Use my location for Google search results and other Google services.

Figure 10: Google Location Screen

5. Navigating the Screens

There are many ways to navigate the Nexus 7. These are just a few of the methods:

- Use the ⬠ key to return to the Home screen at any time. Any application or tool currently in use will be in the same state when it is re-opened.

- Touch the ▭ key to show all applications that have been opened recently. Touch an application to switch to it.

- At the main Home screen, slide your finger to the left or right to access additional Home screens. The Nexus 7 allows you to customize up to five.

- Touch the ⬅ key at any time to return to the previous screen or menu, or to hide the keyboard.

6. Types of Home Screen Objects

Each Home screen on the Nexus 7 is fully customizable. Refer to *"Organizing Home Screen Objects"* on page 25 to learn how to customize the Home screens. Each screen can hold the following items:

- **Widget** - A tool that can be used directly on the Home screen without opening it like an application. Widgets usually take up a fraction or all of the screen, while applications are added as icons. The Books widget is shown in **Figure 11**.

- **Application** - A program that opens in a new window, such as Gmail or a game. Applications are added to the Home screen as icons.

- **Folder** - A folder of application icons or shortcuts.

Note: A folder cannot store widgets.

Figure 11: Books Widget

7. Organizing Home Screen Objects

Customize the Home screens by adding, deleting, or moving objects. Refer to *"Types of Home Screen Objects"* on page 23 to learn more about them. To add an object to a Home screen:

1. Touch the ⊞ icon at the bottom of any Home screen. A list of all installed applications and widgets appears, as shown in **Figure 12**. Touch the screen and flick left to view a list of widgets. Flick your finger to the right to view applications again.
2. Touch and hold an application or widget icon. The Home screen you were previously viewing appears.
3. Release the screen. The object is placed in the selected location on the Home screen.

Note: If you are returned to the list of installed applications and widgets, then you have tried to place the object on a Home screen that does not have sufficient space. The message "No more room on this Home screen" will also appear at the bottom of the screen. Refer to the following hints to learn how to create space on a Home screen.

There are multiple ways to clean up the Home screens. Use the following tips to clean up Home screens:

- To remove objects from the Home screen, touch and hold the object until **Remove** appears at the top of the screen. Move the object over **Remove** and release the screen. The object is removed from the Home screen. It will still appear in the list of installed applications. Refer to *"Uninstalling an Application"* on page 43 to learn how.

- To move an object, touch and hold it until **Remove** appears at the top of the screen. Move the object to the desired location and release the screen to place it. Move the object to the edge of the screen to move it to another Home screen.

- To create a folder, touch and hold an application icon and drag it on top of another. To add more icons to an existing folder, drag the icons on top of the existing folder. To remove an icon from a folder, touch and hold it, drag it anywhere outside the folder, and release the screen.

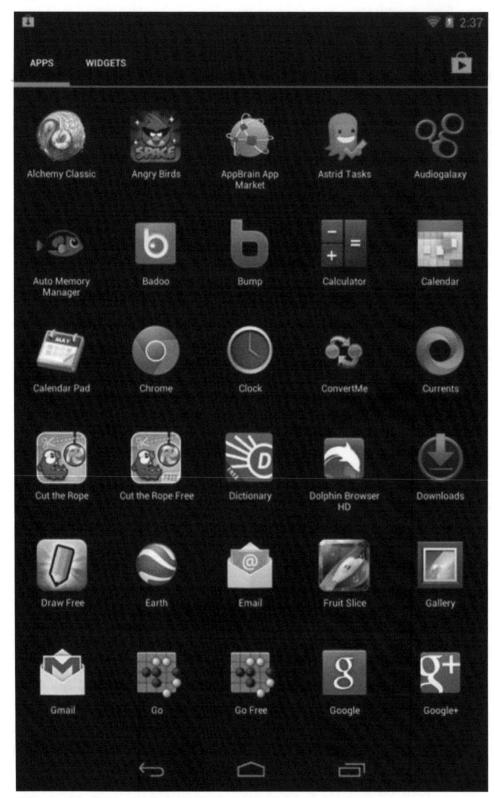

Figure 12: List of All Installed Applications and Widgets

8. Exporting and Importing Files Using a PC or Mac

You can import files to the Nexus 7 from a computer, such as images and documents. You can also export files from the tablet to a computer. To export and import files using a PC or Mac:

1. Connect the Nexus 7 to your PC or Mac using the provided USB cable. "Connected as a media device" appears at the top of the tablet's screen. If you are using a Mac, download the Android File Transfer application at **www.android.com/filetransfer/** before proceeding.

2. Double-click the icon in the Computer folder, as outlined in **Figure 13**, if using a PC. On a Mac, open the Android File Transfer program. The Nexus 7 folder opens. To access the Computer folder on a PC, click the button and then click **Computer** in Windows Vista or later. Double-click **My Computer** on the desktop in Windows 95 or later.

3. Double-click **Internal storage**. The Internal Storage folder opens on a PC, as shown in **Figure 14**, or on a Mac, as shown in **Figure 15**.

4. Double-click a folder inside the Internal Storage folder to view its contents. The folder opens.

5. Click and drag a file into the folder from your computer, or drag one to your computer from the Nexus 7 folder. The file is transferred.

Note: Operating systems prior to Windows Vista may not be able to recognize the Nexus 7 when it is connected.

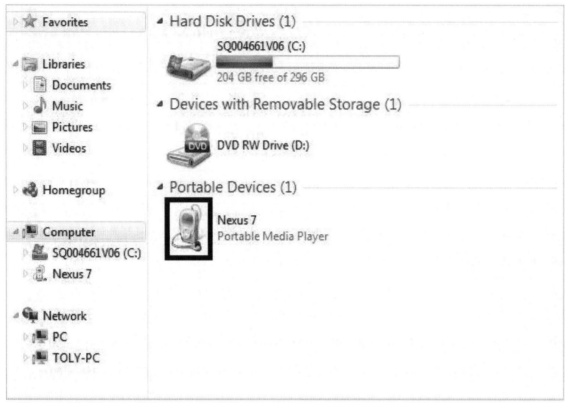

Figure 13: Nexus 7 Icon on a PC

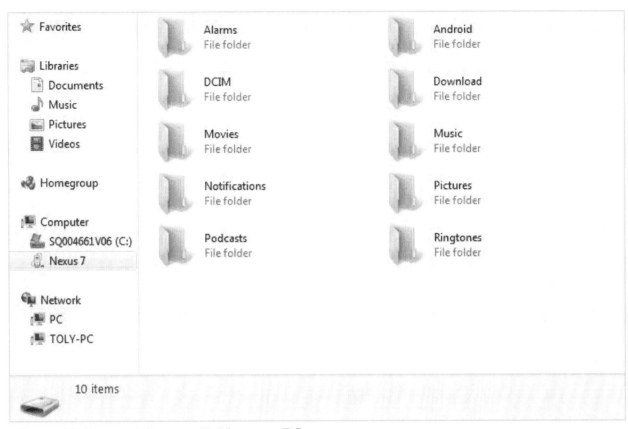

Figure 14: Internal Storage Folder on a PC

Figure 15: Internal Storage Folder on a Mac

Managing Applications

Table of Contents

1. Setting Up a Google Account

In order to buy applications, you will need to assign a Google account to the Nexus 7. Refer to *"Setting Up the Gmail Application"* on page 73 to learn how to assign a Google account to the device.

2. Searching for Applications

There are two ways to search for applications: perform a manual search or browse them by category.

Manual Search

To search for an application manually, type in a keyword or phrase.

1. Touch the [icon] icon on the Home screen, or touch the [icon] icon and then touch the [icon] icon. The Play Store opens, as shown in **Figure 1**.
2. Touch the [icon] icon at the top of the screen. The Search field and the keyboard appear.
3. Type the name of an application or developer and touch the [icon] key. All matching results appear, as shown in **Figure 2**.
4. Touch **Apps** in the upper left-hand corner of the screen, as outlined in **Figure 2**. The Application results appear.
5. Touch the name of an application. A description of the application appears. Refer to *"Purchasing Applications"* on page 38 to learn how to buy the selected application.

Browse by Category

View applications by genre, such as games, travel, or productivity. To browse applications by category:

1. Touch the [icon] icon on the Home screen, or touch the [icon] icon and then touch the [icon] icon. The Play Store opens.
2. Touch **Apps** on the left-hand side of the screen, as outlined in **Figure 1**. The Featured Applications screen appears, as shown in **Figure 3**.
3. Touch the screen and move your finger to the right. A list of application categories appears, as shown in **Figure 4**.
4. Touch a category. The top applications in the selected category appear, as shown in **Figure 5**.
5. Touch the name of an application. A description of the application appears. Refer to *"Purchasing Applications"* on page 38 to learn how to buy the selected application.

Note: Some applications, such as games, may have sub-categories (i.e. racing, puzzle, arcade). For these cases, repeat steps 3 and 4 to browse the sub-categories.

Figure 1: Play Store

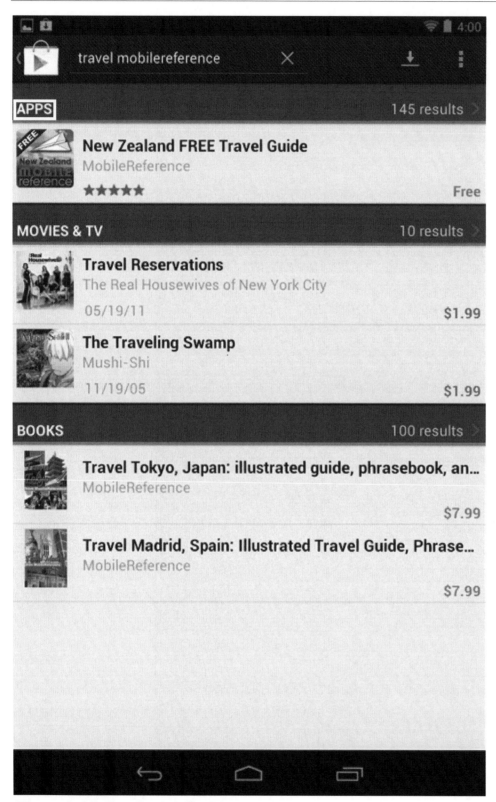

Figure 2: Market Search Results

Figure 3: Featured Applications Screen

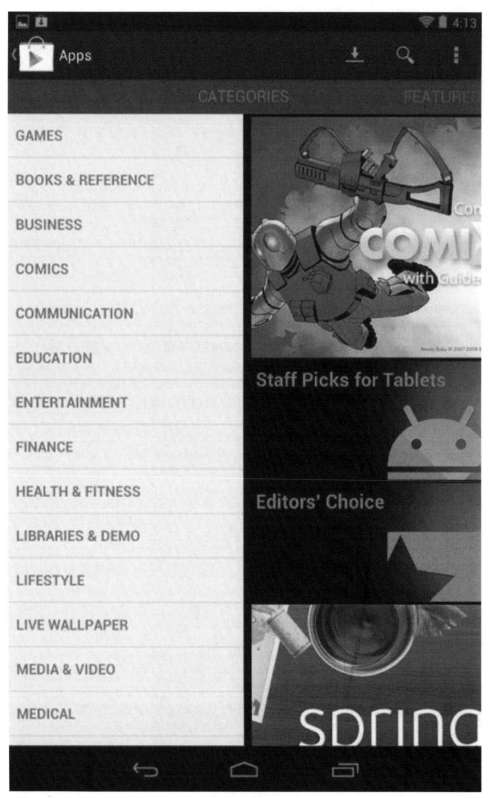

Figure 4: List of Application Categories

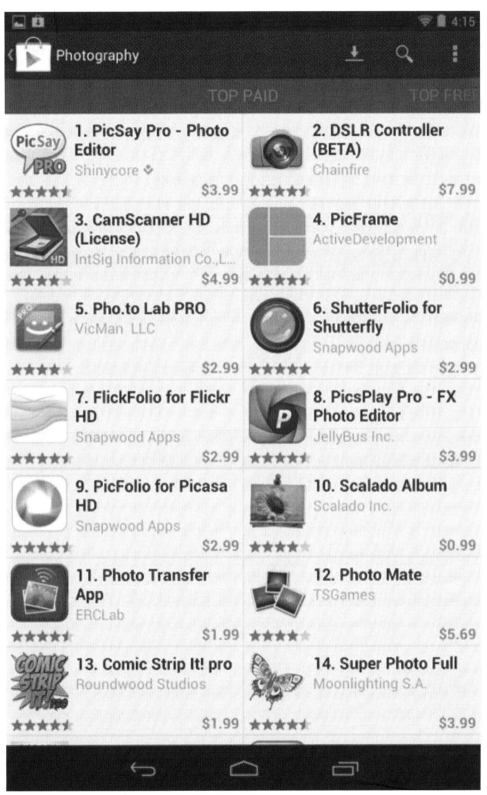

Figure 5: List of Applications in a Category

3. Purchasing Applications

Applications can be purchased directly from the Nexus 7 using the Play Store. To buy an application:

1. Touch the ▶ icon on the Home screen, or touch the ⊞ icon and then touch the ▶ icon. The Play Store opens.
2. Find the application that you wish to purchase. Refer to *"Searching for Applications"* on page 32 to learn how.
3. Touch the name of an application. The Application Description screen appears, as shown in **Figure 6** (free application) and **Figure 7** (paid application).
4. Follow the appropriate instructions below to download the application:

Installing Free Applications

1. Touch the Install button. The Permissions window appears, as shown in **Figure 8**.
2. Touch the Accept & download button. The application is downloaded and installed. The download progress is shown on the Application Description screen while the application is downloading.
3. Touch the Open button. The application opens. Refer to *"Types of Home screen Objects"* on page 23 and *"Organizing Home screen Objects"* on page 25 to learn more about accessing applications.

Installing Paid Applications

1. Touch the price of the application. A warning appears regarding the application's access to various parts of the Nexus 7. Touch **OK** at the bottom left of the screen.
2. Enter your credit card information, which Google Checkout requests the first time that you purchase an application. The information is saved and the Purchase Confirmation screen appears. On all subsequent purchases, the Purchase screen appears, as shown in **Figure 9**.
3. Touch the Accept & buy button. The application is purchased, downloaded, and installed. The download progress is shown on the Application Description screen while the application is downloading.
4. Touch the Open button. The application opens. Refer to *"Types of Home screen Objects"* on page 23 and *"Organizing Home screen Objects"* on page 25 to learn more about accessing applications.

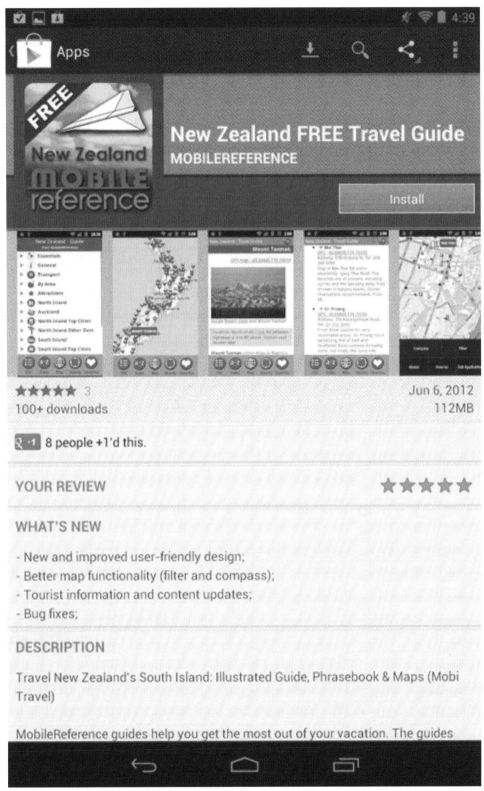

Figure 6: Application Description Screen (Free Application)

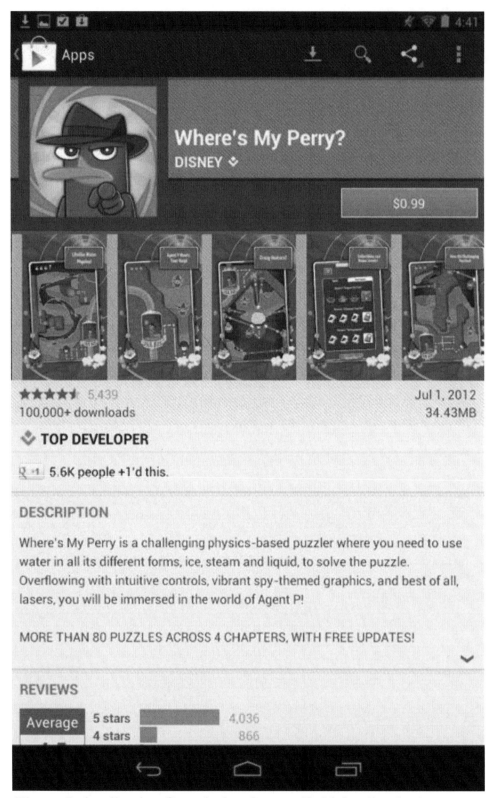

Figure 7: Application Description Screen (Paid Application)

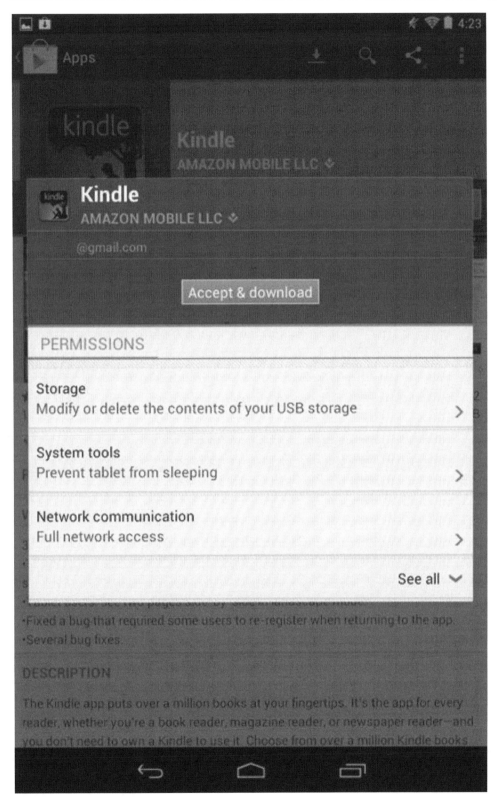

Figure 8: Permissions Window

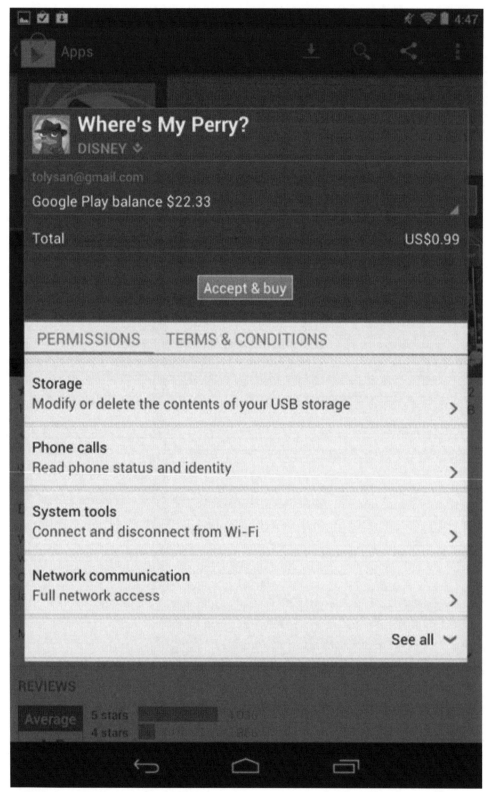

Figure 9: Purchase Screen

4. Uninstalling an Application

Within the first 15 minutes of purchasing an application, it can be uninstalled for a full refund. After 15 minutes have passed, the following instructions only apply to uninstalling an application with no refund. To uninstall an application:

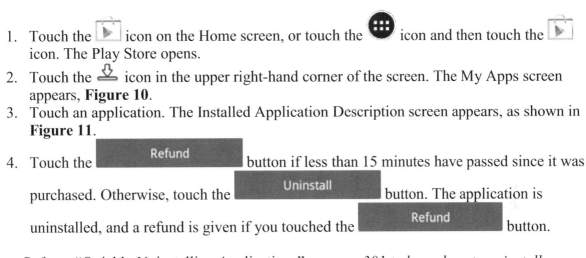

1. Touch the ![icon] icon on the Home screen, or touch the ⊕ icon and then touch the ![icon] icon. The Play Store opens.
2. Touch the ⬇ icon in the upper right-hand corner of the screen. The My Apps screen appears, **Figure 10**.
3. Touch an application. The Installed Application Description screen appears, as shown in **Figure 11**.
4. Touch the [Refund] button if less than 15 minutes have passed since it was purchased. Otherwise, touch the [Uninstall] button. The application is uninstalled, and a refund is given if you touched the [Refund] button.

Note: Refer to "Quickly Uninstalling Applications" *on page 301 to learn how to uninstall an application without opening the Play Store.*

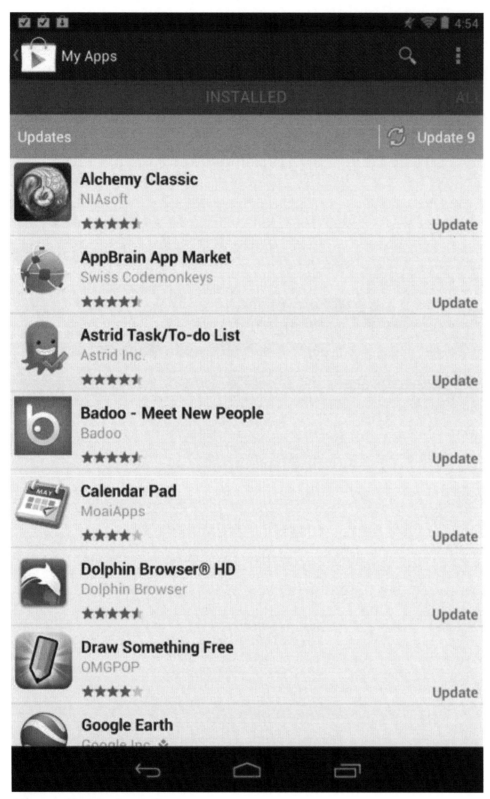

Figure 10: My Apps Screen

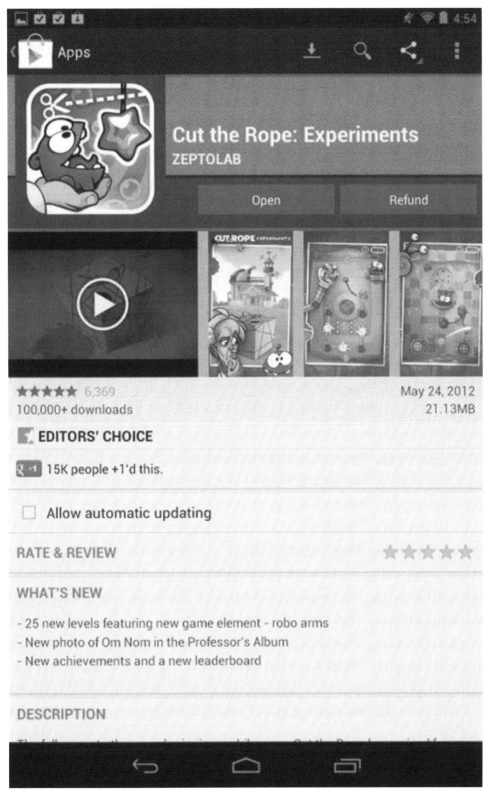

Figure 11: Installed Application Description Screen

5. Sharing an Application via Email

The Nexus 7 allows you to share applications with friends via email. When sharing an application, a link to the application's page in the Play Store is sent. Those with whom links are shared will still need to pay for the shared applications that they purchase. To share an application via email:

1. Touch the ▶ icon on the Home screen, or touch the ⊞ icon and then touch the ▶ icon. The Play Store opens.
2. Find the application that you wish to share. If you already own the application that you wish to share, touch the ⬇ icon in the upper right-hand corner of the screen to browse your installed applications. Otherwise, refer to *"Searching for Applications"* on page 32 to learn how to find an application for sale in the Play Store.
3. Touch the name of an application. The Application Description screen appears, as shown in **Figure 12**.
4. Touch the ◀ icon in the upper right-hand corner of the screen, as outlined in **Figure 12**, if this is your first time sharing an application. A list of Sharing options appears. If this is not your first time sharing an application, touch the ✉ icon in the upper right-hand corner of the screen, as outlined in **Figure 12**.
5. Touch the ✉ icon in the list of Sharing options. A new email is composed with a link to the shared application pasted into the message, as shown in **Figure 13**.
6. Enter the recipient's email address. The email address is entered.
7. Touch the ➤ button in the upper right-hand corner of the screen, as outlined in **Figure 13**. The email is sent, sharing the application with the selected recipient.

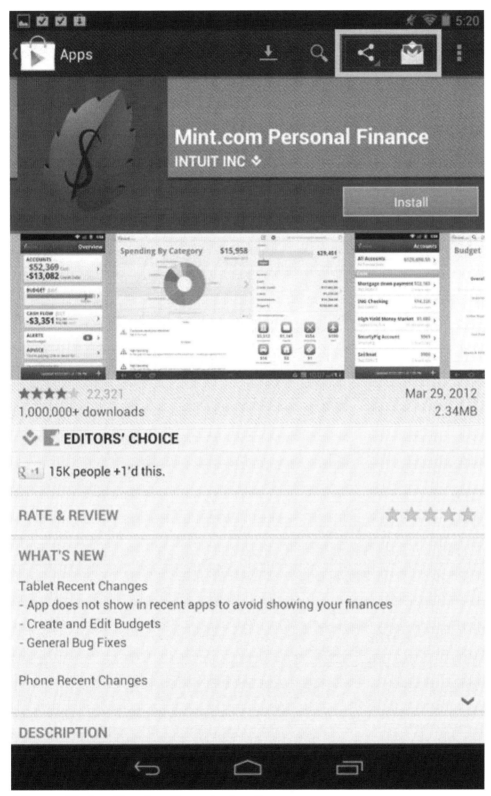

Figure 12: Application Description Screen

Figure 13: New Email with a Link to the Shared Application

6. Closing Applications Running in the Background

Most applications will keep running in the background even after they are exited, and some require a considerable amount of memory and battery life. To speed up the performance of the Nexus 7 and conserve battery life, try closing some or all of these applications while they are not in use. To close an application running in the background, touch the ⬚ key at any time. The Open Applications screen appears, as shown in **Figure 14**. Touch an application and slide your finger to the left or right. The application is closed.

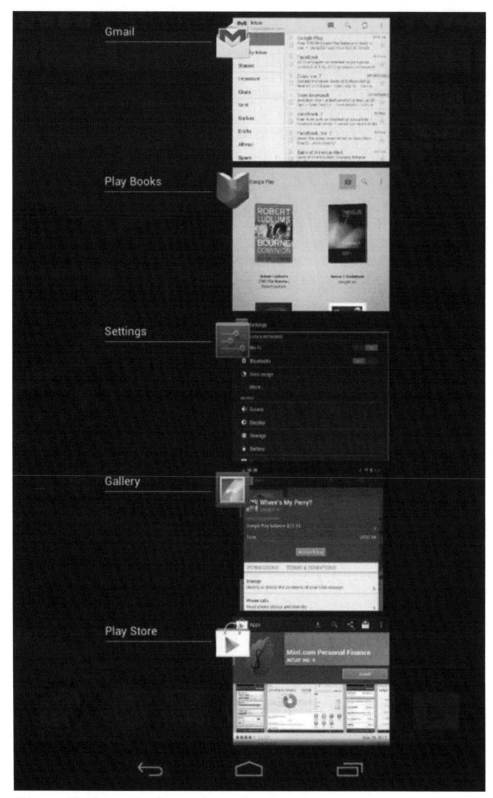

Figure 14: Recently Opened Applications Screen

7. Reading User Reviews

Reading user reviews may help when making a decision between similar applications from different developers. To read user reviews for an application:

1. Touch the ▶ icon on the Home screen, or touch the ⊞ icon and then touch the ▶ icon. The Play Store opens.
2. Find an application. Refer to *"Searching for Applications"* on page 32 to learn how.
3. Touch the name of the application. The Application Description screen appears.
4. Touch the screen and move your finger up to scroll to the bottom of the page. The reviews for the current application are found below the 'What's New' or 'Description' section, as outlined in **Figure 15**.

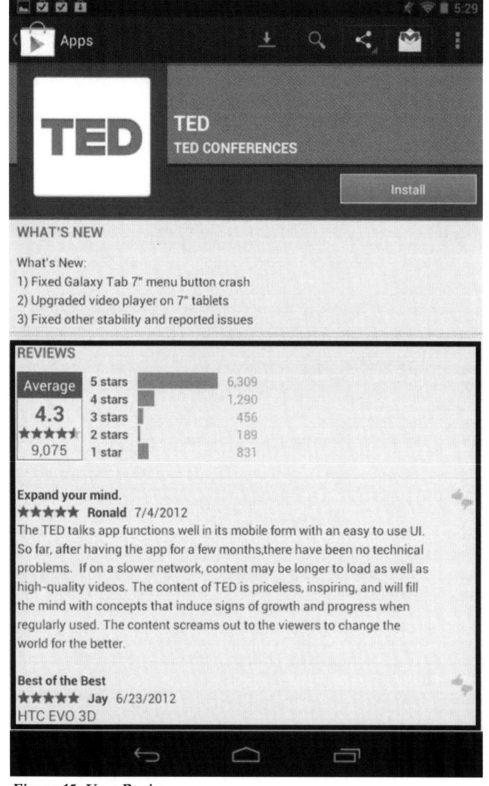

Figure 15: User Reviews

Managing Photos

Table of Contents

1. Taking Pictures

While the Nexus 7 has a 1.2 megapixel front-facing camera, the tablet does not come with a dedicated Camera application. Instead, you will need to download a camera application from the Play Store. Refer to *"Taking Pictures and Capturing Video"* on page 303 to learn how. Refer to *"Purchasing Applications"* on page 38 to learn more about downloading applications.

2. Browsing Pictures

You can browse captured or saved photos using the Gallery application. To view the images stored on your device:

1. Touch the ![icon] icon on the Home screen, or touch the ![icon] icon and then touch the ![icon] icon. The Gallery opens and album thumbnails are displayed, as shown in **Figure 1**.
2. Touch an album. The album opens. The photos in the album appear as thumbnails by default, as shown in **Figure 2**.
3. Touch the screen and move your finger to the left or right. Other photos in the album appear.
4. Touch a photo. The image appears in Full-Screen mode. Touch the ![back key] key to return to the album.

Figure 1: Gallery

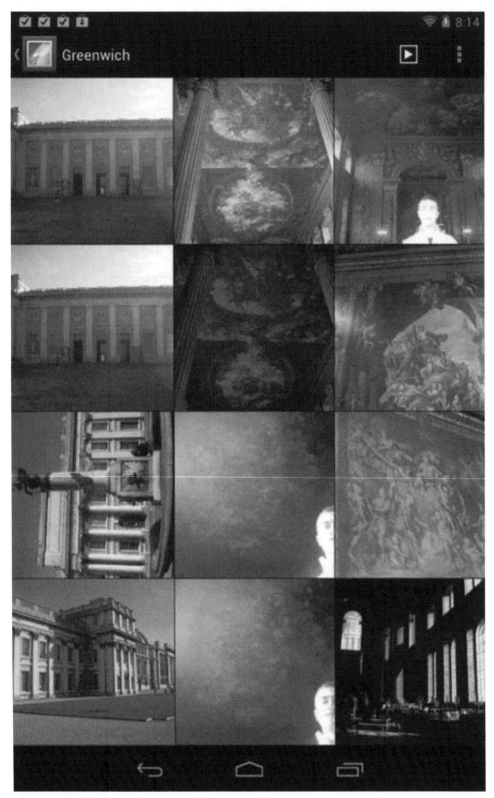

Figure 2: Photo Thumbnails in an Album

3. Starting a Slideshow

The Nexus 7 can play slideshows using the pictures stored in the Gallery. To start a slideshow:

1. Touch the ▨ icon on the Home screen, or touch the ⦿ icon and then touch the ▨ icon. The Gallery opens and thumbnails for multiple albums appear.
2. Touch an album thumbnail to open it. The photos in the album appear as thumbnails.
3. Touch the ▶ icon in the upper right-hand corner of the screen. The slideshow begins, displaying the photos from the selected album in Full-Screen view.
4. Touch the screen once. The slideshow stops.

4. Applying Special Effects to Pictures

Pictures stored on the Nexus 7 can be cropped, rotated, and enhanced with various effects. To edit a picture:

1. Open a photo. The image appears in full-screen mode. Refer to *"Browsing Pictures"* on page 54 to learn how to open an image.
2. Touch the ▤ icon in the upper right-hand corner of the screen. The Photo Editing menu appears, as shown in **Figure 3**.
3. Touch **Edit**. The photo is opened for editing, as shown in **Figure 4**. Follow the steps in the appropriate section below to learn how to use the various editing options:

Adjusting the Lighting Effects

There are several options that allow you to adjust the amount of light in an image. To adjust the Lighting effects:

1. Follow the instructions above. Then, touch the ◣ icon at the bottom of the screen. The Lighting options appear, as shown in **Figure 5**.
2. Touch one of the options in the list. The Lighting Adjustment bar appears, as shown in **Figure 6**.
3. Touch the ◯ slider and drag it to the left or right to decrease or increase the effect, respectively. The lighting effect is applied.
4. Touch **Save** in the upper right-hand corner of the screen. The photo is saved as a separate image in the same album as the original.

Adding Special Effects

There are several special effects that may be applied to a photo, such as "Film Grain" and "Posterize." To add a special effect:

1. Follow the instructions at the beginning of this section. Then, touch the ![FX] icon at the bottom of the screen. The Special Effects menu appears, as shown in **Figure 7**.
2. Touch an effect in the list. The effect is applied to the photo. Some effects will cause an adjustment bar to appear. Touch the ◎ slider and drag it to the left or right to decrease or increase the effect, respectively.
3. Touch **Save** in the upper right-hand corner of the screen. The photo is saved as a separate image in the same album as the original.

Adjusting the Color Effects

There are several color effects that may be applied to a photo, such as "Black and White" and "Negative." To add a color effect:

1. Follow the instructions at the beginning of this section. Then, touch the ![icon] icon at the bottom of the screen. The Color Effects menu appears, as shown in **Figure 8**.
2. Touch an effect in the list. The effect is applied to the photo. Some effects will cause an Adjustment bar to appear. Touch the ◎ slider and drag it to the left or right to decrease or increase the effect, respectively.
3. Touch **Save** in the upper right-hand corner of the screen. The photo is saved as a separate image in the same album as the original.

Note: Touch the ![back key] *key at any time to undo the most recent applied effect. If the* ![back key] *key is not available, no effects have been applied.*

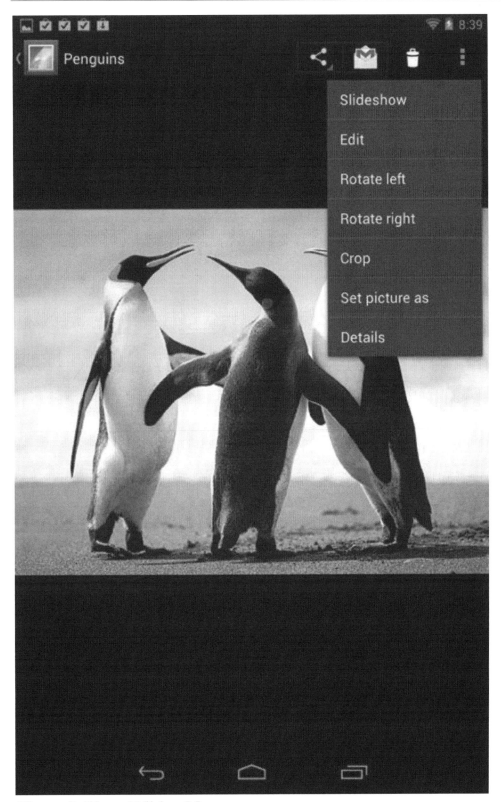

Figure 3: Photo Editing Menu

Figure 4: Photo Opened for Editing

Figure 5: Lighting Options

Figure 6: Lighting Adjustment Bar

Figure 7: Special Effects Menu

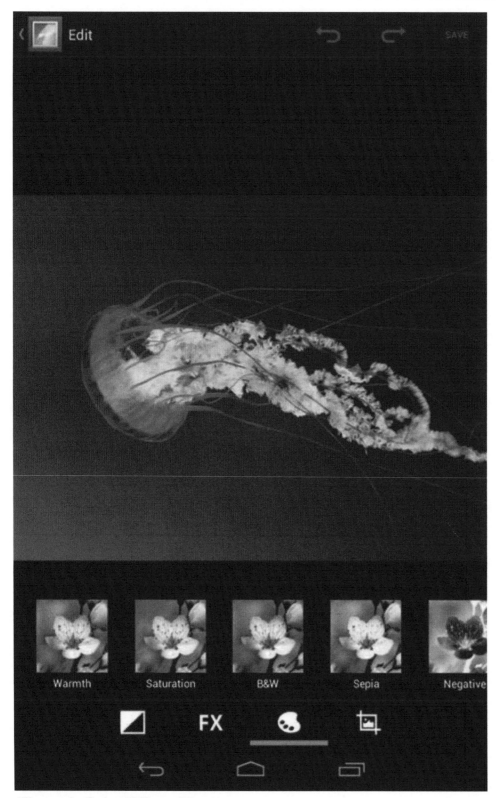

Figure 8: Color Effects Menu

5. Cropping a Picture

You may crop a photo to use a specific piece of it. To crop a photo:

1. Open a photo. Refer to *"Browsing Pictures"* on page 54 to learn how to open an image.

2. Touch the ▢ icon in the upper right-hand corner of the screen. The Photo Editing menu appears.

3. Touch **Edit**. The photo is opened for editing.

4. Touch the ▣ icon. The Photo Adjustment menu appears, as shown in **Figure 9**.

5. Touch the ⬚ icon. The cropping markers appear on the photo, as shown in **Figure 10**.

6. Touch the ● sliders on the photo and drag to resize the crop. The crop is resized.

7. Touch inside the blue rectangle and drag it around to select the portion of the photo that you would like to use. The portion of the photo is selected.

8. Touch **Save** in the upper right-hand corner of the screen. The photo is saved as a separate image in the same album as the original.

Figure 9: Photo Adjustment Menu

Figure 10: Cropping Markers on a Photo

6. Flipping or Rotating a Picture

You may rotate a photo in 90 degree increments, or flip it to view it upside down or as a mirror image. To flip or rotate a picture:

1. Open a photo. Refer to *"Browsing Pictures"* on page 54 to learn how to open an image.
2. Touch the ⬚ icon in the upper right-hand corner of the screen. The Photo Editing menu appears.
3. Touch **Edit**. The photo is opened for editing.
4. Touch the ⬚ icon. The Photo Adjustment menu appears.
5. Scroll to the right and touch the ⟳ icon or the ⬚ icon. The photo is enabled for rotation or flipping, respectively.
6. Touch the photo and move your finger in any direction to rotate or flip the photo. The photo is flipped or rotated in the direction indicated.
7. Touch **Save** in the upper right-hand corner of the screen. The photo is saved as a separate image in the same album as the original.

7. Enhancing Facial Features in a Picture

You may enhance a photo by adding more light or a tan to the faces in it, or by removing red eyes. To enhance the facial features in a picture:

1. Open a photo. Refer to *"Browsing Pictures"* on page 54 to learn how to open an image.

2. Touch the ⬚ icon in the upper right-hand corner of the screen. The Photo Editing menu appears.

3. Touch **Edit**. The photo is opened for editing.

4. Touch the 🖼 icon. The Photo Adjustment menu appears.

5. Touch one of the following icons to enhance facial features:

👓 - Adds more light to the faces in the picture.

🙂 - Adds an artificial tan to the faces in the picture.

👁 - Removes red eyes from the faces in the picture, an issue which is caused by the reflection of the flash off the retinas. Touch each eye to remove the red eye effect.

6. Touch **Save** in the upper right-hand corner of the screen. The photo is saved as a separate image in the same album as the original.

8. Sharpening a Picture

If you wish to see more detail in a photo, you may wish to sharpen it. To sharpen a picture:

1. Open a photo. Refer to *"Browsing Pictures"* on page 54 to learn how to open an image.
2. Touch the ▤ icon in the upper right-hand corner of the screen. The Photo Editing menu appears.
3. Touch **Edit**. The photo is opened for editing.
4. Touch the ▣ icon. The Photo Adjustment menu appears.
5. Scroll to the right and touch the ▣ icon. The Sharpening adjustment bar appears.
6. Touch the ◯ slider and drag it to the right or left to make the photo more or less sharp, respectively. The photo is sharpened.
7. Touch **Save** in the upper right-hand corner of the screen. The photo is saved as a separate image in the same album as the original.

9. Deleting Pictures

Warning: Once a picture is deleted, there is no way to restore it.

To free up some space in the Nexus 7's memory, try deleting some pictures from the Gallery. To delete a picture:

1. Touch the ▨ icon on the Home screen, or touch the ⊞ icon and then touch the ▨ icon. The Gallery opens.
2. Touch an album. The album opens and the photos are displayed in thumbnail view.
3. Touch and hold a photo. The photo is selected and highlighted.
4. Touch the 🗑 icon in the upper right-hand corner of the screen. A confirmation dialog appears.
5. Touch **OK**. The photo is deleted.

Note: You may not delete pictures that belong to a Picasa album. Every Picasa album has a ◉ *icon in the lower left-hand corner of the album thumbnail. Delete photos in Picasa albums using the Picasa application.*

10. Importing and Exporting Pictures Using a PC or Mac

Pictures and other files can be transferred to and from the Nexus 7. Refer to *"Exporting and Importing Files Using a PC or Mac"* on page 27 to learn how.

Using the Gmail Application

Table of Contents

1. Setting Up the Gmail Application

Before the Gmail application can be used, a Google account must be registered to the Nexus 7. If you followed all of the instructions in *"Performing First-Time Setup"* on page 16, then you already have a Google account and you may skip this section. To add your Google account to the Nexus 7:

1. Touch the icon on the Home screen, or touch the icon and then touch the icon. The Settings screen appears, as shown in **Figure 1**.
2. Scroll down and touch **Add account** under 'Accounts'. The Add Account window appears, as shown in **Figure 2**.
3. Touch **Google**. The Add Google Account screen appears, as shown in **Figure 3**.
4. Touch **Existing** if you already have a Google account. The Google Sign In screen appears, as shown in **Figure 4**. Otherwise, touch **New** to create a new Google account. Once the account is created, it will be added to the device automatically, and you may skip the rest of the steps in this section. If you would like to create your Google account using the Web browser on your computer, navigate to **https://accounts.google.com/NewAccount** to do so.
5. Enter your Gmail address and password and touch the button. The Google+ screen appears.
6. Touch **Not now** to skip this step for now. The Entertainment screen appears. Otherwise, touch **Join Google+** to join the social network.
7. Touch **Not now** to skip the Entertainment screen for now. A confirmation screen appears and your Google account is added to the Nexus 7. Otherwise, touch **Set up credit card** on the Entertainment screen to add a credit card in order to have the ability to purchase content from the Play Store.

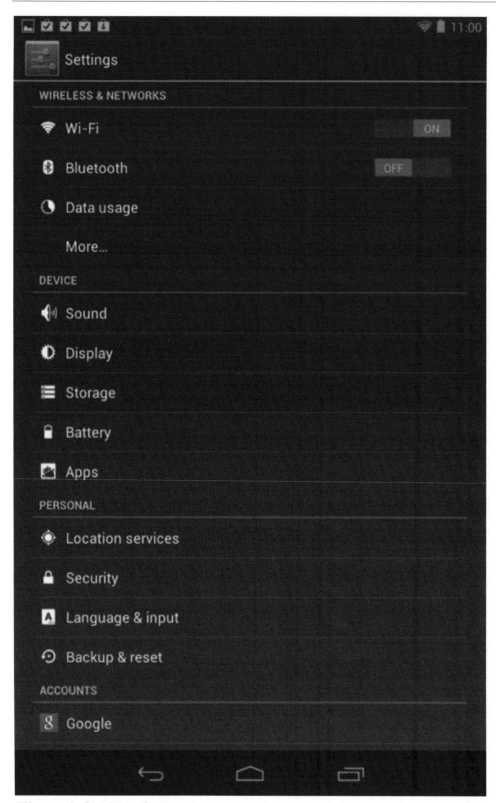

Figure 1: Settings Screen

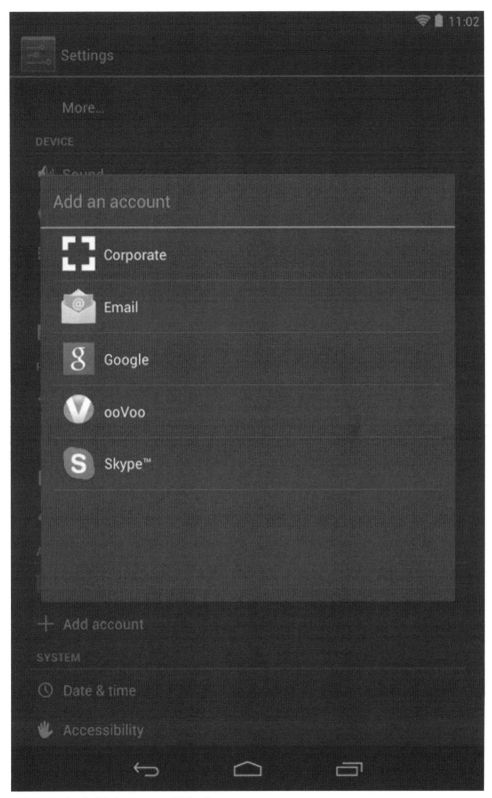

Figure 2: Add Account Window

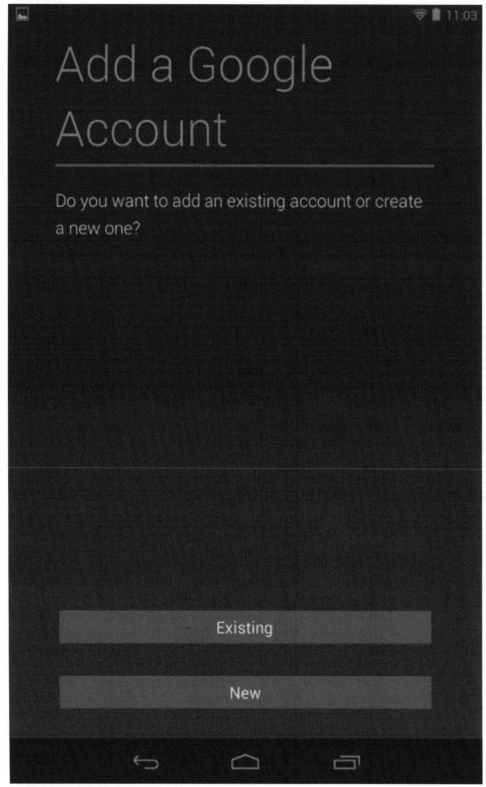

Figure 3: Add Google Account Screen

Figure 4: Google Sign In Screen

2. Reading Email

Since the Nexus 7 is completely synced with every Google product, it is highly recommended to use a Gmail account on the device. To read email using your Gmail account:

1. Touch the ![icon] icon on the Home screen, or touch the ![icon] icon and then touch the ![icon] icon. The Gmail application opens and the Inbox appears, as shown in **Figure 5**.
2. Touch an email. The email opens.
3. Touch the screen and move your finger to the left or right to view the previous email or next email, respectively (where "previous" refers to an older email and "next" refers to a newer one).
4. To switch to a different account at any time, touch your email address in the upper left-hand corner of the screen, as outlined in **Figure 5**. The email addresses associated with existing Gmail accounts currently registered to the Nexus 7 appear.
5. Touch an account name. The mailboxes associated with the account appear.

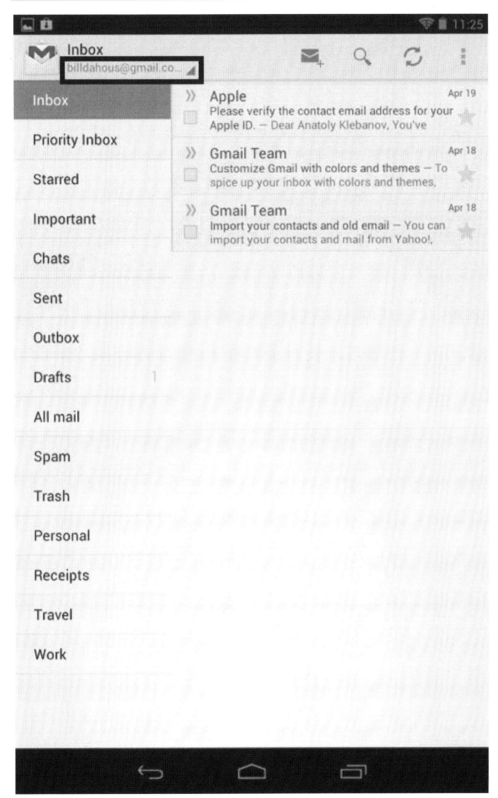

Figure 5: Gmail Application Inbox

3. Writing an Email

Compose email directly from the Nexus 7 using the Gmail application. To write an email:

1. Touch the ![M] icon on the Home screen, or touch the ![⋮] icon and then touch the ![M] icon. The Gmail application opens.
2. Touch the ![✉+] icon in the upper right-hand corner of the screen, as outlined in **Figure 6**. The Compose screen appears, as shown in **Figure 7**.
3. Start typing a name or email address. If the email address is stored in contacts, recipient suggestions appear while typing, as shown in **Figure 8**.
4. Touch the 'Subject' field and enter the topic of the email. Touch the 'Compose email' field and type the message. The message is entered.
5. Touch the ![►] button in the upper right-hand corner of the screen, as outlined in **Figure 7**. The email is sent.

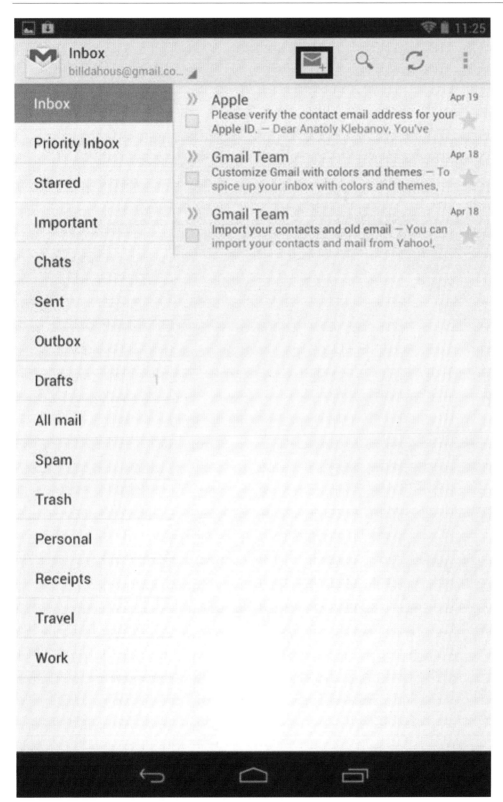

Figure 6: Compose Icon Outlined

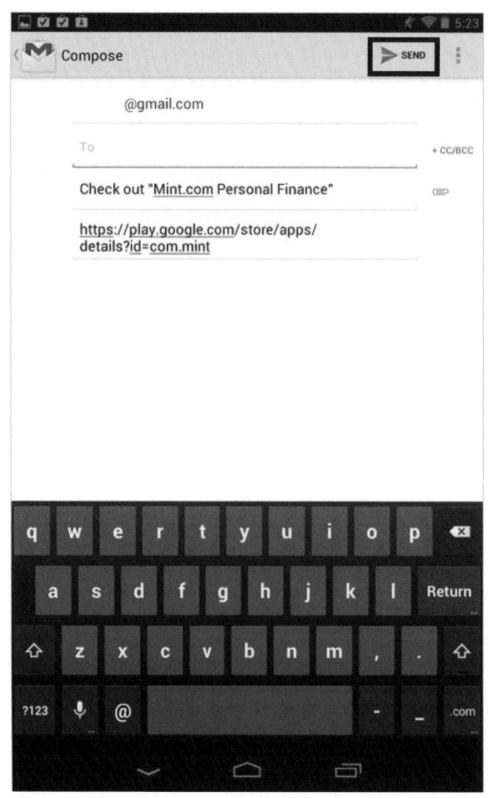

Figure 7: Compose Screen

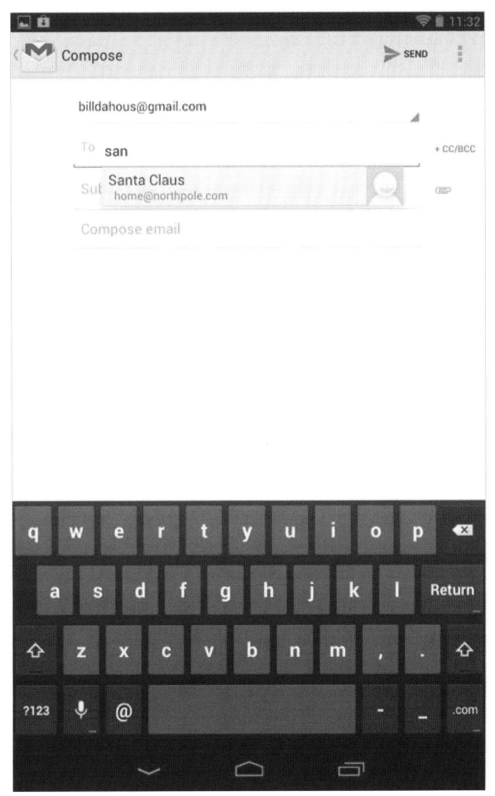

Figure 8: Recipient Suggestions

4. Replying to and Forwarding Emails

After receiving an email in the Gmail application, a direct reply can be sent, or the email can be forwarded. To reply to or forward an email:

1. Touch the ![M] icon on the Home screen, or touch the ● icon and then touch the ![M] icon. The Gmail application opens.
2. Touch an email. The email opens.
3. Touch one of the following icons to perform the associated action, as outlined in **Figure 9**.

![reply icon] - Send a reply to the sender.

![reply all icon] - Send a reply to all recipients.

![forward icon] - Forward the email to a third party.

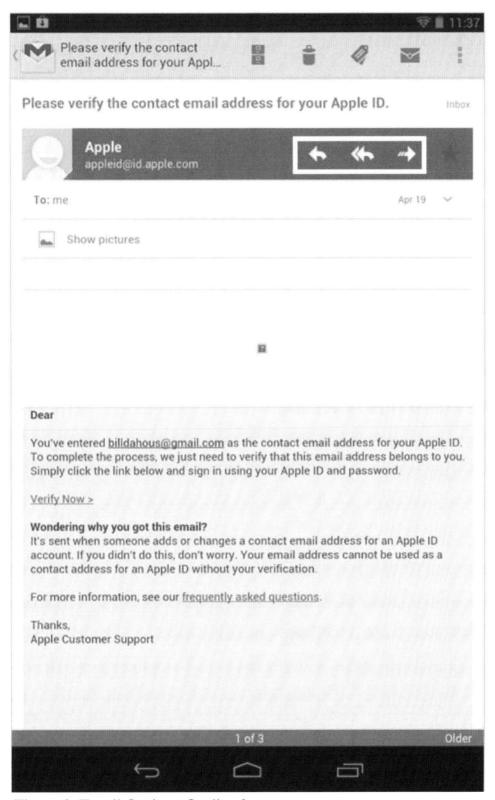

Figure 9: Email Options Outlined

5. Deleting and Archiving Emails

Deleting an email sends it to the Trash folder. To completely delete an email, the Trash folder must then be emptied using a Web browser (not covered in this guide). Otherwise, email will be automatically deleted from the Trash folder after 30 days. To delete an email:

1. Touch the ![icon] icon on the Home screen, or touch the ![icon] icon and then touch the ![icon] icon. The Gmail application opens.
2. Touch an email. The email opens.
3. Touch the ![icon] icon at the top of the screen, as outlined in **Figure 10**. The email is moved to the Trash folder. Touch **Undo** in the lower right-hand corner of the screen to return the email to the Inbox. The 'Undo' option is no longer available if you open another email or exit the Gmail application.

To clean up the Inbox without deleting emails, try archiving them. Archiving an email removes it from the Inbox and places it in the All Mail folder. To archive an email:

1. Touch the ![icon] icon on the Home screen, or touch the ![icon] icon and then touch the ![icon] icon. The Gmail application opens.
2. Touch an email. The email opens.
3. Touch the ![icon] icon. The email is archived. Touch **Undo** in the lower right-hand corner of the screen to return the email to the Inbox. The 'Undo' option is no longer available if you open another email or exit the Gmail application.

*Note: To find an archived email, touch **All Mail** on the left side of the screen while viewing your Inbox.*

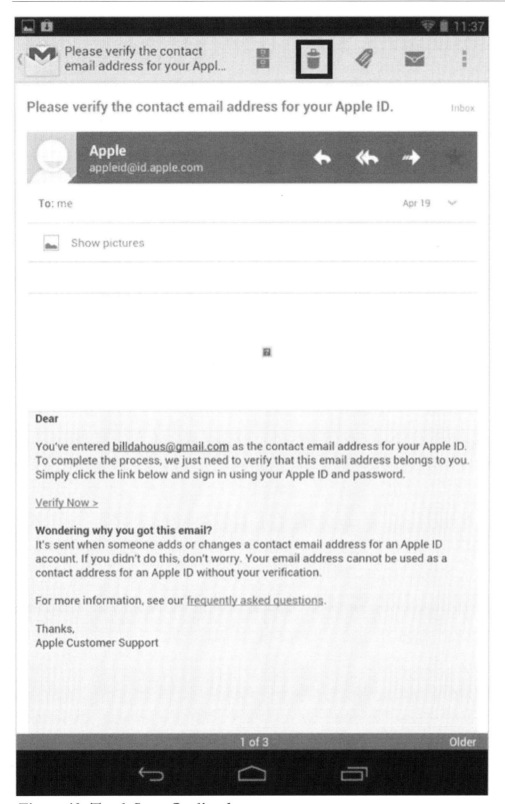

Figure 10: Trash Icon Outlined

6. Adding Labels to Emails

Emails can be classified according to the nature of the message, such as 'Work' or 'Personal'. To add a label to an email:

1. Touch the ⊠ icon on the Home screen, or touch the ⊕ icon and then touch the ⊠ icon. The Gmail application opens.
2. Touch an email. The email opens.
3. Touch the ✐ icon at the top of the screen, as outlined in **Figure 11**. The Labels dialog appears, as shown in **Figure 12**.
4. Touch a label to add it to the email. A ☑ mark appears next to each selected label.
5. Touch a label again to deselect it. The label is deselected and the ☑ mark disappears.
6. Touch **OK**. The selected labels are assigned to the email.

Note: Touch a label under 'All Labels' or 'Recent Labels' on the left side of the Inbox to view the emails assigned to that label.

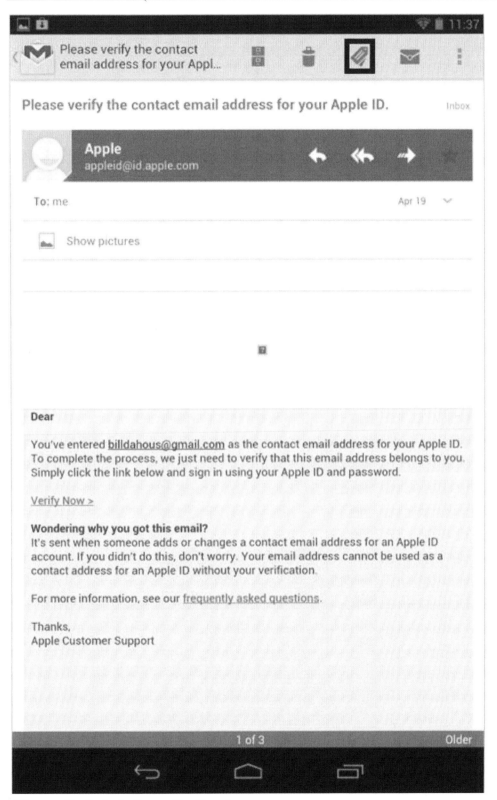

Figure 11: Labels Icon Outlined

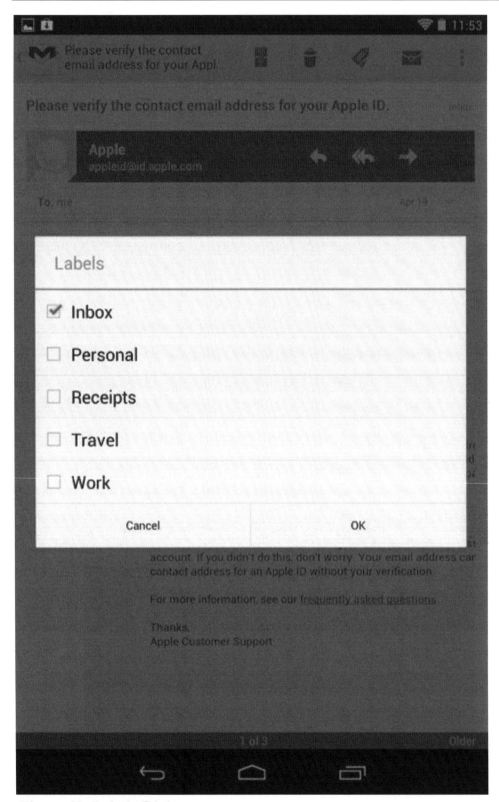

Figure 12: Labels Dialog

7. Searching the Inbox

To find an email in the Inbox, use the Search function, which searches email addresses, message text, and subject lines. To search the Inbox:

1. Touch the ![M] icon on the Home screen, or touch the ![⊞] icon and then touch the ![M] icon. The Gmail application opens.
2. Touch the 🔍 icon at the top of the screen. The Search field appears at the top of the screen.
3. Enter a search term and touch the 🔍 key. The Nexus 7 searches the Inbox and the matching results appear.

8. Adjusting the Gmail Settings

The Gmail application has several adjustable settings, such as the default signature, notification tones, and text size. To change these settings:

1. Touch the ![M icon] icon on the Home screen, or touch the ![grid icon] icon and then touch the ![M icon] icon. The Gmail application opens.

2. Touch the ![menu icon] icon in the upper right-hand corner of the screen. The Gmail menu appears, as shown in **Figure 13**.
3. Touch **Settings**. The Gmail Settings screen appears, as shown in **Figure 14**.
4. Touch **General settings**. The General Settings screen appears, as shown in **Figure 15**.
5. Touch one of the following options to perform the corresponding function:

   - **Confirm before deleting** - Display confirmations before deleting emails.

   - **Confirm before archiving** - Display confirmations before archiving emails.

   - **Confirm before sending** - Display confirmations when sending emails.

   - **Auto-advance** - Choose which screen the Gmail application shows after deleting or archiving an email.

   - **Message text size** - Change the size of the text in the emails.

   - **Clear Search History** - Clear the email search history to preserve privacy.

   - **Hide pictures in messages** - Pictures embedded in emails won't display automatically unless you allow them.

From the General Settings screen, touch your email address, and then touch one of the following options to perform the corresponding action:

- **Priority Inbox** - Make the Priority Inbox the default Inbox.

- **Email notifications** - Turn on new Email notifications. The icon appears in the upper left-hand corner of the screen when a new email arrives.

- **Ringtone & vibrate** - Displays the Manage Labels screen, where you can choose which mailboxes display new email notifications and select the sound that plays when a new email arrives. Touch **Ringtone** on the Manage Labels screen to select the Notification ringtone.

- **Signature** - Enter a default signature that will be attached to the end of each sent email.

- **Gmail sync is ON** - View the Accounts & Sync screen, where you can manage email accounts.

- **Days of mail to sync** - Choose how many days in the past the Inbox should sync. For instance, if you select '3', the Gmail application will go back three days each time it syncs the email.

- **Manage Labels** - Brings you to the same screen as 'Ringtone & vibrate'.

- **Download attachments** - Turn on to have Gmail automatically download any attached files.

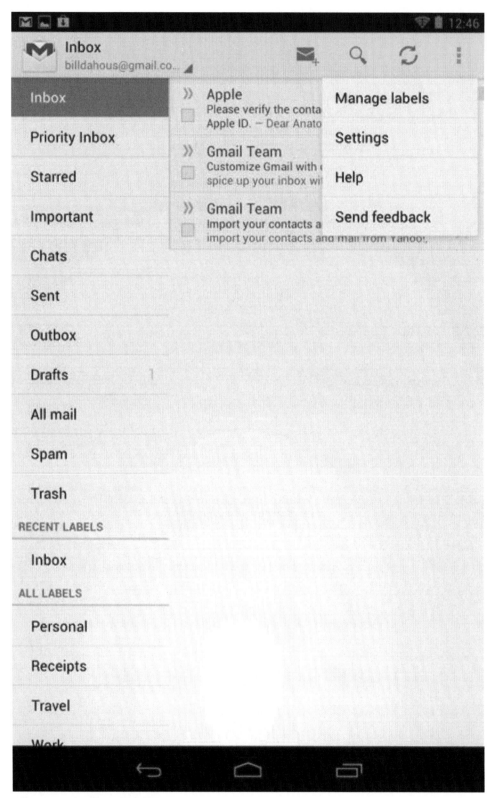

Figure 13: Gmail Menu

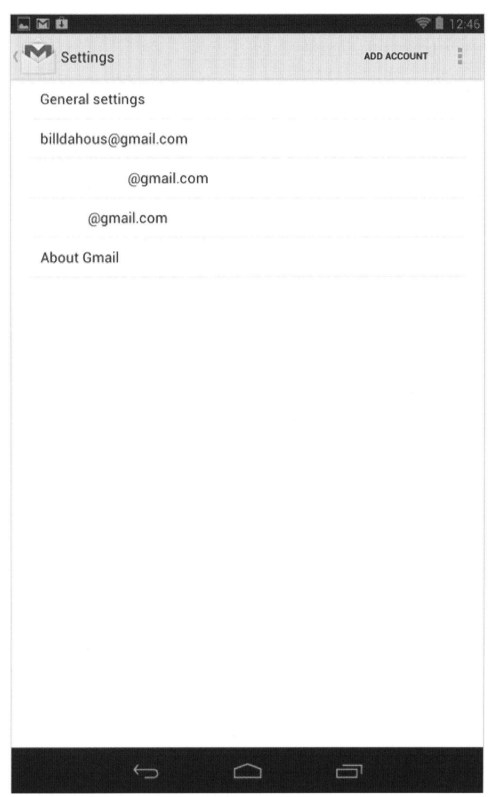

Figure 14: Gmail Settings Screen

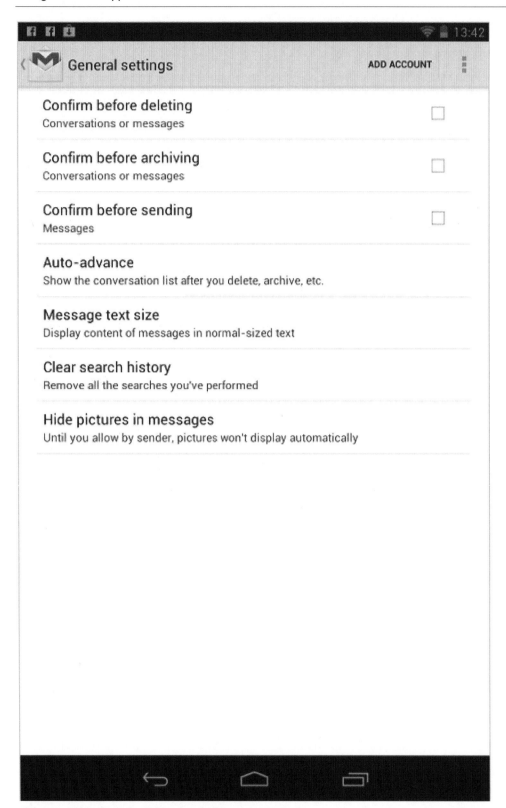

Figure 15: General Settings Screen

Making Voice and Video Calls

Table of Contents

1. Downloading Skype for Voice and Video Calling

To make voice and video calls on the Nexus 7, download the Skype application. To download the Skype application:

1. Touch the [▶] icon on the Home screen, or touch the ⊞ icon and then touch the [▶] icon. The Play Store opens, as shown in **Figure 1**.

2. Touch the 🔍 icon at the top of the screen. The Search field and the keyboard appear.

3. Enter **Skype** and touch the ↵ key. A list of search results appears.

4. Touch **Skype**. The Skype description appears.

5. Touch the **Install** button. The Permissions window appears, as shown in **Figure 2**.

6. Touch the **Accept & download** button. The Skype application is downloaded and installed.

7. Touch the Ⓢ icon on the Home screen, or touch the ⊞ icon and then touch the Ⓢ icon. The Skype application opens and the Skype Welcome screen appears, as shown in **Figure 3**. If the Welcome screen looks different, then you have downloaded the wrong application.

Note: The Skype application is free, so do not fall for paid mimics.

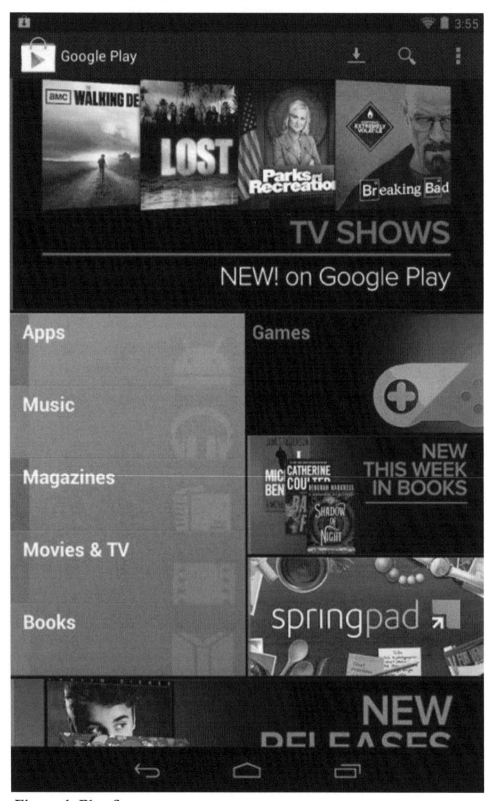

Figure 1: Play Store

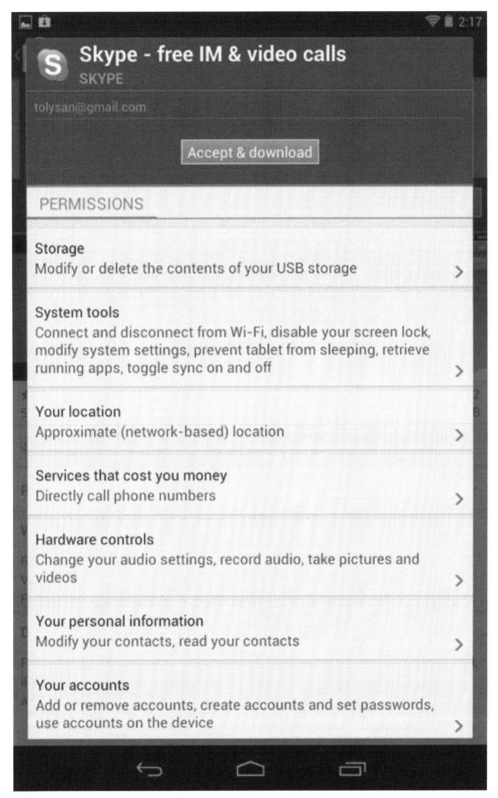

Figure 2: Permissions Window

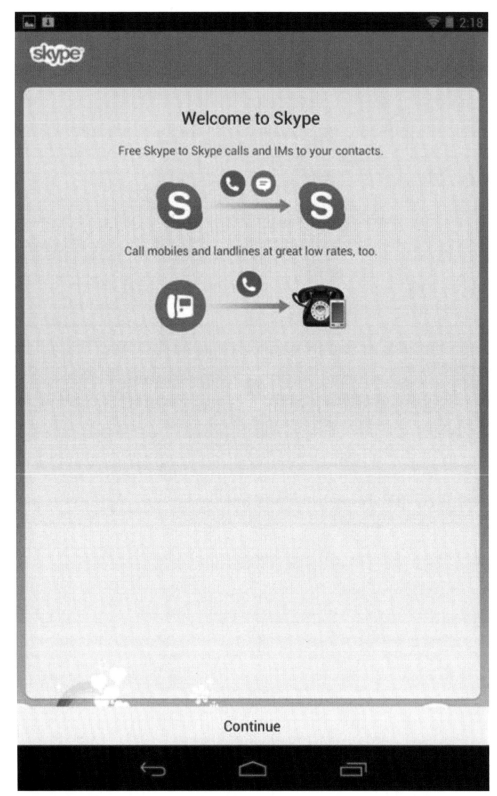

Figure 3: Skype Welcome Screen

2. Setting Up Skype

Before making voice calls, set up Skype with your own account. If you do not have a Skype account, navigate to **https://login.skype.com/account/signup-form** to create one, or touch **Create an account** in step 4 below. To set up Skype:

1. Touch the icon. The Skype application opens.
2. Touch **Continue** at the bottom of the screen. The Terms and Conditions appear.
3. Touch **Accept** at the bottom of the screen. The Skype Login screen appears, as shown in **Figure 4**.
4. Enter your login information and touch **Sign In**. The Skype application logs in to your account.

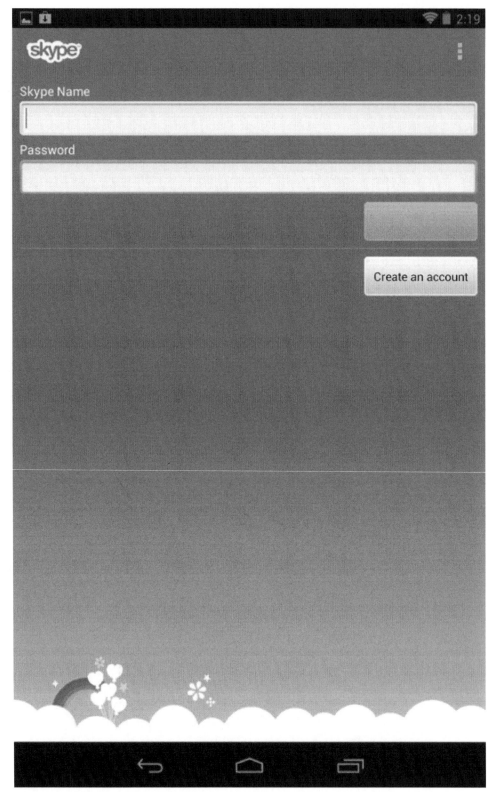

Figure 4: Skype Login Screen

3. Managing Skype Contacts

The Skype application can store Skype names and phone numbers in the Address Book.

To add a new contact to the Address Book:

1. Touch the ![icon] icon on the Skype Home screen. The Address Book appears, as shown in **Figure 5**.
2. Touch the ![icon] icon in the upper right-hand corner of the screen. A search field appears at the top of the screen.
3. Touch the search field at the top of the screen. The virtual keyboard appears.
4. Enter the contact's Skype name. Skype searches for the contact in its directory and all matching search results appear as you type.
5. Touch the name of the contact in the list. The contact's information appears.
6. Touch **Add**. The keyboard appears and the message "Hi, I'd like to add you as a contact on Skype." appears automatically.
7. Edit the message if you desire. Touch the Add contacts button at the bottom of the screen. When the contact accepts your invitation, you will be able to see their status in your Address Book.

To remove a contact from the Address Book:

1. Touch the ![icon] icon on the Skype Home screen. The Address Book appears.
2. Touch and hold a contact. The Contact menu appears, as shown in **Figure 6**.
3. Touch **Remove contact**. A confirmation window appears.
4. Touch **Yes**. The contact is removed from your Skype Address Book.

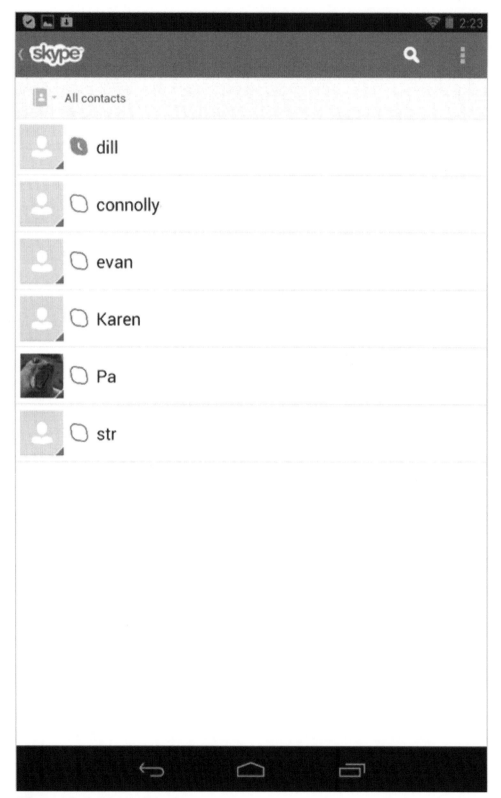

Figure 5: Address Book

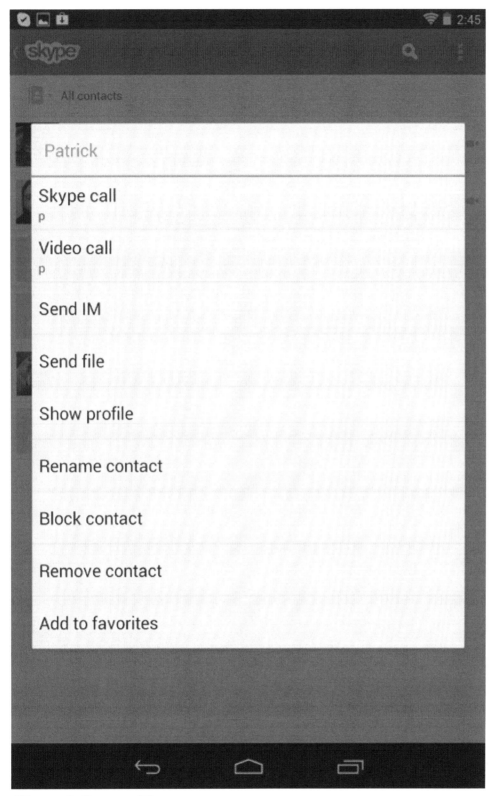

Figure 6: Contact Menu

4. Making a Voice Call

Use Skype to make voice calls to phone numbers or other Skype users. Note that calling a phone number, whether it is mobile or land line, is not free.

To make a voice call to a mobile phone or land line:

1. Touch the ![dialpad icon] icon on the Skype Home screen. The dialpad appears, as shown in **Figure 7**.

2. Dial the phone number that you wish to call and touch the ![Call button] button at the bottom of the screen. The dialpad is hidden. If your account has no money in it, the Skype Credit window appears, as shown in **Figure 8**. To add funds, touch **Buy credit** at the bottom of the screen. Otherwise, the call is connected (provided that the recipient answers) and the Voice Call screen appears, as shown in **Figure 9**.
3. Touch the ![end call button] button to end the call. The call is ended.

Note: One free call is allowed before adding funds to your Skype account for the first time.

To make a voice call to a Skype contact:

1. Touch the ![contact icon] icon on the Skype Home screen. The Address Book appears.
2. Touch a contact. The Contact Information screen appears, as shown in **Figure 10**.
3. Touch **Voice call**. Skype calls the contact and the Skype Call screen appears, as shown in **Figure 11**.
4. Touch the ![end call button] button to end the call. The call is ended.

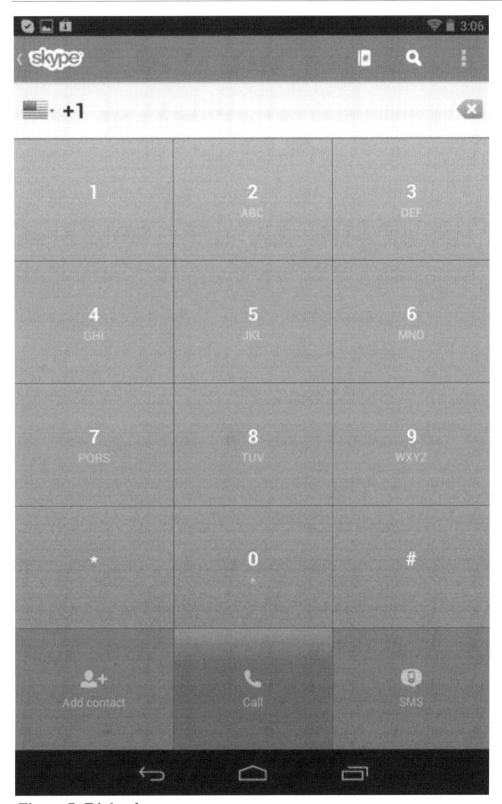

Figure 7: Dialpad

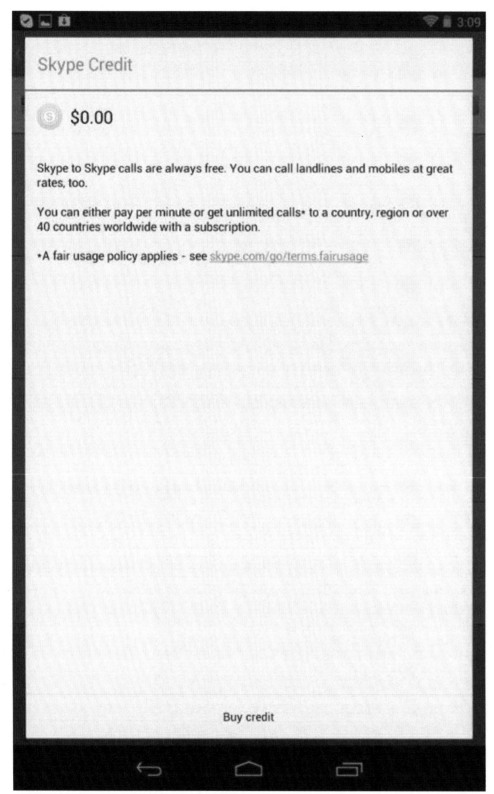

Figure 8: Skype Credit Window

Figure 9: Voice Call Screen

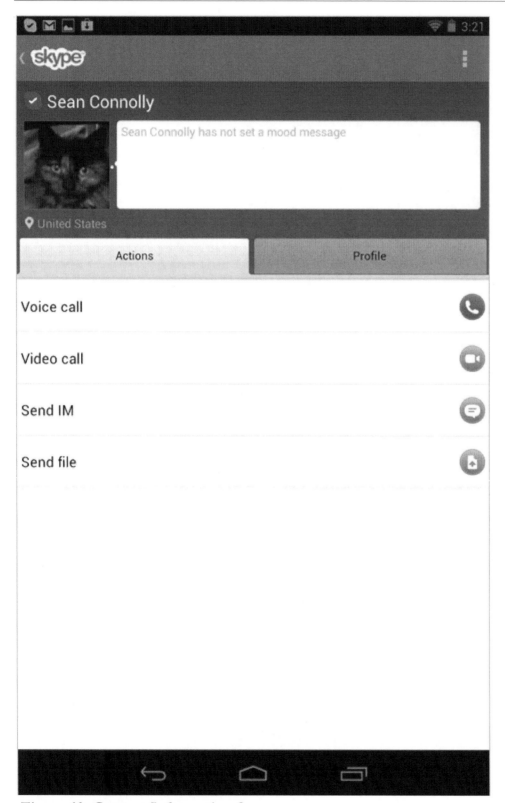

Figure 10: Contact Information Screen

Figure 11: Skype Call Screen

5. Making a Video Call

Use Skype to make video calls to other Skype users. To make a video call using Skype:

1. Touch the icon on the Skype Home screen. The Address Book appears.
2. Touch a contact in the list. The Contact Information screen appears.
3. Touch **Video call**. Skype initiates a video call.
4. Touch the button to end the call. The call is ended.

Managing Contacts

Table of Contents

1. Adding a New Contact

On the Nexus 7, a contact can be added to the Address Book in your linked Google account. Adding a contact to a Google account allows total syncing of contacts across your Nexus 7 and your online account. To add a new contact:

1. Touch the 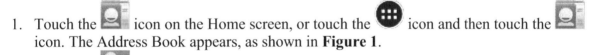 icon on the Home screen, or touch the icon and then touch the icon. The Address Book appears, as shown in **Figure 1**.
2. Touch the 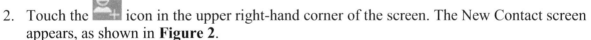 icon in the upper right-hand corner of the screen. The New Contact screen appears, as shown in **Figure 2**.
3. Enter all desired information by touching each field to enter text. Touch **Done** in the upper left-hand corner of the screen. The contact is stored.

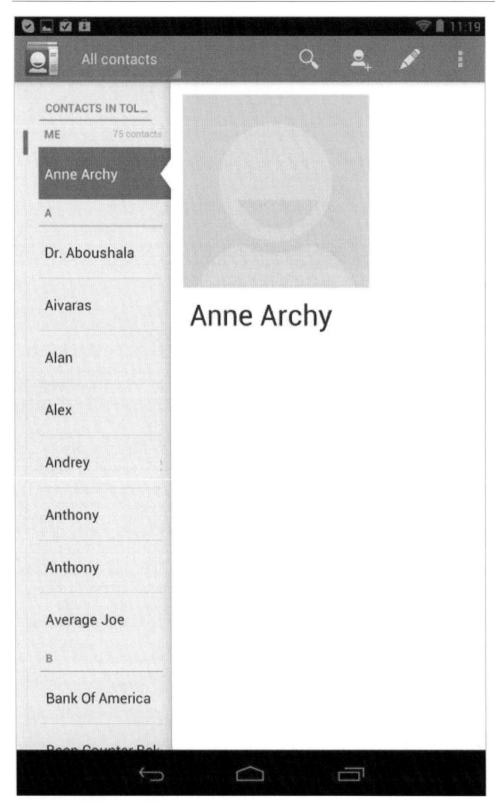

Figure 1: Address Book

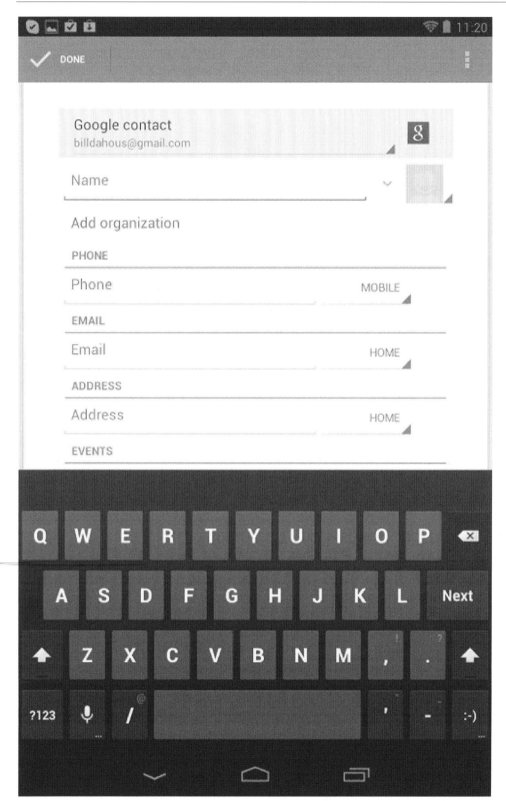

Figure 2: New Contact Screen

2. Creating a Shortcut to a Contact

The fastest way to consistently find a stored contact is to add a shortcut to the contact right to the Home screen. To create a shortcut to a contact:

1. Touch the ![icon] icon on the Home screen, or touch the ● icon and then touch the ![icon] icon. The Address Book appears.
2. Touch the name of the contact that you wish to add to the Home screen. The contact's information appears on the right side of the screen.
3. Touch the blue ![icon] icon in the upper right-hand corner of the screen. The Contact menu appears, as shown in **Figure 3**.
4. Touch **Place on Home screen**. A shortcut to the contact's information is added to the first available Home screen. The Contact shortcut may look similar to the icon outlined in **Figure 4** if there is a picture assigned to the contact. If there is no picture assigned, the ![icon] icon is shown.

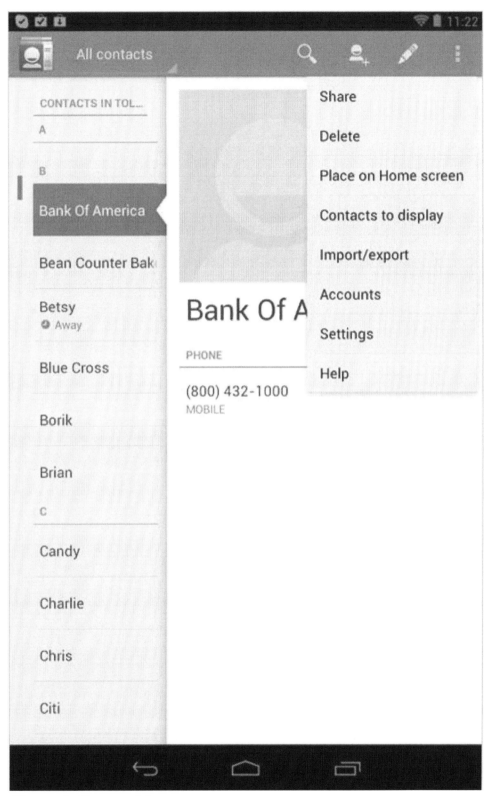

Figure 3: Contact Menu

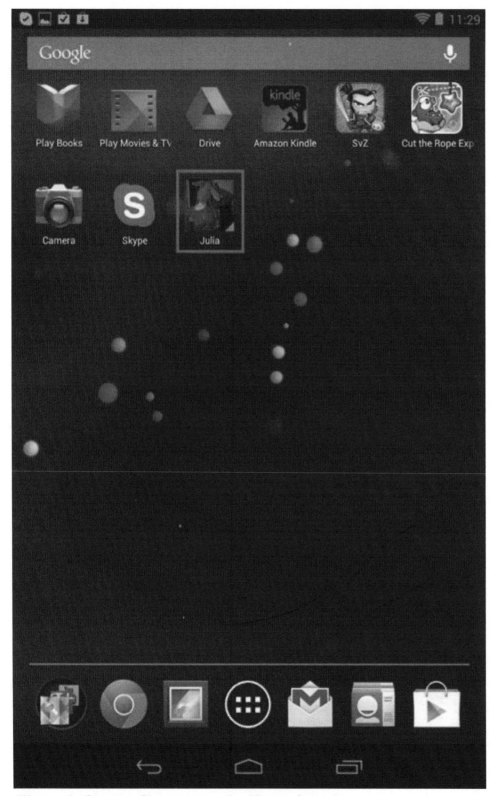

Figure 4: Contact Shortcut on the Home Screen

3. Editing Contact Information

Edit a contact entry to add additional information, such as an email address or alternate phone number. To edit existing contact information:

1. Touch the icon on the Home screen, or touch the icon and then touch the icon. The Address Book appears.
2. Touch the name of the contact that you wish to edit. The contact's information appears on the right side of the screen.
3. Touch the icon in the upper right-hand corner of the screen. The Contact Editing screen appears, as shown in **Figure 5**.
4. Touch a field to edit it. The field is selected.
5. Touch **Done** in the upper left-hand corner of the screen when you are finished editing. The new information is stored in the Address Book.

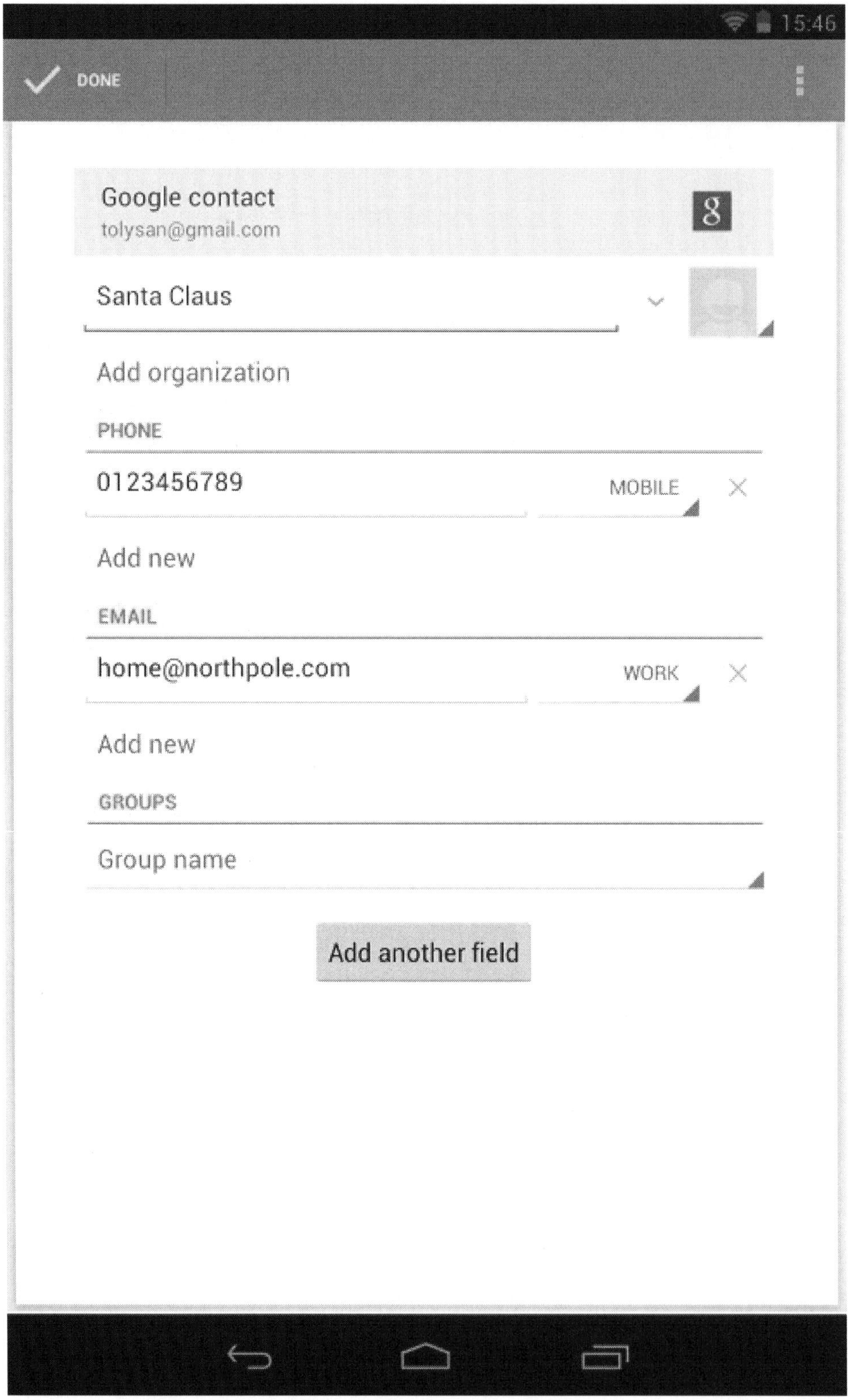

Figure 5: Contact Editing Screen

4. Deleting a Contact

Free up memory on the Nexus 7 by deleting contact information from the Address Book when it is no longer needed. To delete an unwanted contact:

Warning: Contacts cannot be retrieved once they are deleted. Before deleting a contact, make sure that you do not need the information.

1. Touch the [icon] icon on the Home screen, or touch the [icon] icon and then touch the [icon] icon. The Address Book appears.
2. Touch a contact's name in the list on the left-hand side of the screen. The contact's information appears on the right-hand side of the screen.
3. Touch the blue [icon] icon in the upper right-hand corner of the screen. The Contact menu appears.
4. Touch **Delete**. A confirmation dialog appears.
5. Touch **OK**. The contact is deleted.

5. Adding a Contact to a Group

Contacts can be organized into groups for easier browsing. To add a contact to a group:

1. Touch the ![icon] icon on the Home screen, or touch the ● icon and then touch the ![icon] icon. The Address Book appears.
2. Touch the name of the contact that you wish to add to a group. The contact's information appears on the right-hand side of the screen.
3. Touch the ![icon] icon in the upper right-hand corner of the screen. The Contact Editing screen appears.
4. Touch **Group name** under 'GROUPS', as outlined in **Figure 6**. A list of available groups appears, as shown in **Figure 7**.
5. Touch the names of the groups to which the contact should be assigned. A ![checkmark] mark appears next to each selected group. You may also touch **Create new group** to create your own. After a group has been created, it will appear in the list of available groups.
6. Touch the name of a group in the list that has a ![checkmark] mark next to it. The ![checkmark] mark disappears and the contact will not be added to the group or will be removed from the group.
7. Touch **Done** in the upper left-hand corner of the screen. The contact is added to or removed from the selected groups.

To view the list of groups at any time:

1. Touch **All contacts** in the upper left-hand corner of the Address Book screen, as outlined in **Figure 8**. The Address Book options appear.
2. Touch **Groups**. A list of the existing groups appears on the left-hand side of the screen, as shown in **Figure 9**.
3. Touch one of the groups in the list. The contacts that belong to the group appear on the right-hand side of the screen.

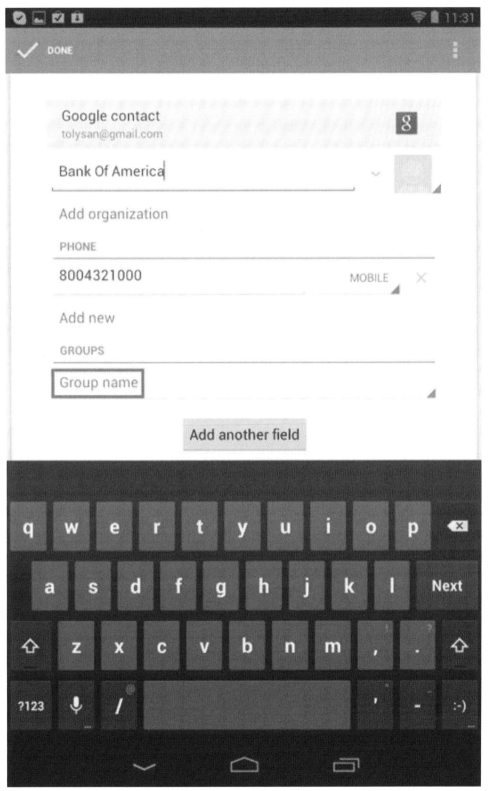

Figure 6: Group Name Outlined

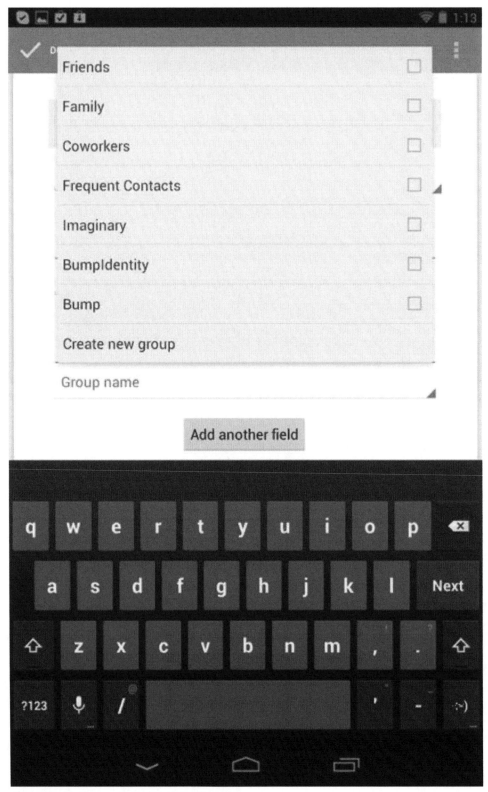

Figure 7: List of Available Groups

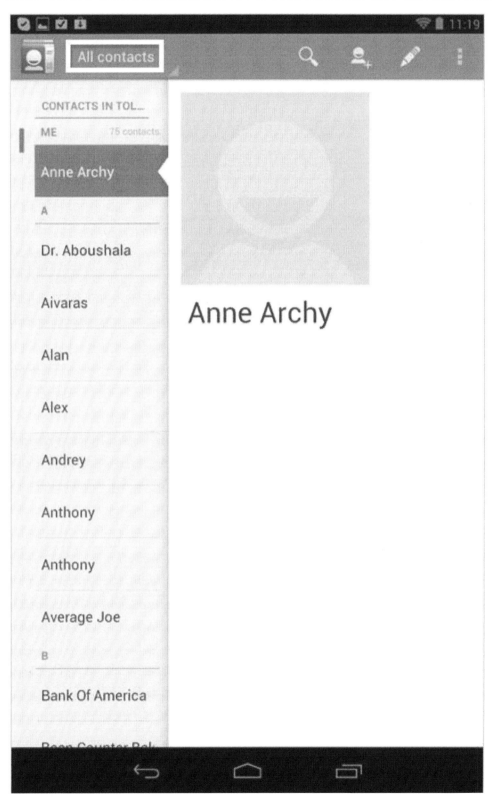

Figure 8: 'All contacts' Outlined

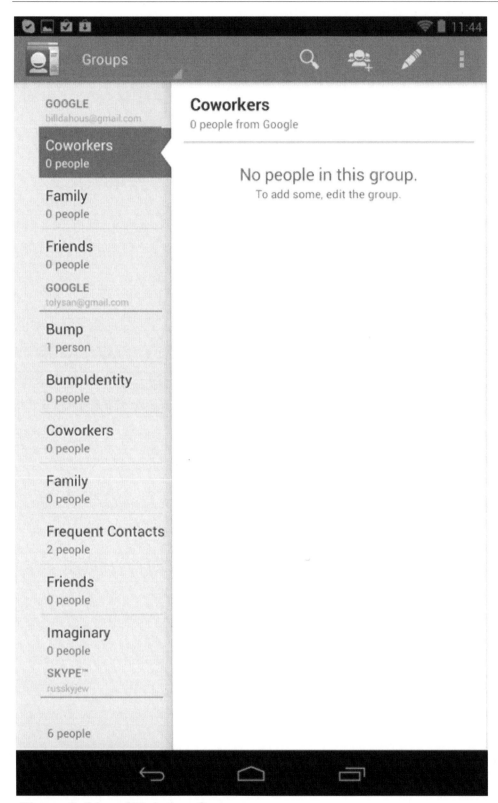

Figure 9: List of Existing Groups

6. Adding a Contact to Favorites

The Favorites group can be used to quickly access the people you contact the most often. To add a contact to Favorites:

1. Touch the [icon] icon on the Home screen, or touch the [icon] icon and then touch the [icon] icon. The Address Book appears.
2. Touch a contact's name. The contact's information appears on the right side of the screen.
3. Touch the [icon] icon to the right of the contact's name, as outlined in **Figure 10**. The contact is added to Favorites.

Note: To access your Favorites, touch **All contacts** *in the upper left-hand corner of the Address Book screen. The Address Book menu appears. Touch* **Favorites**. *The Favorites list appears.*

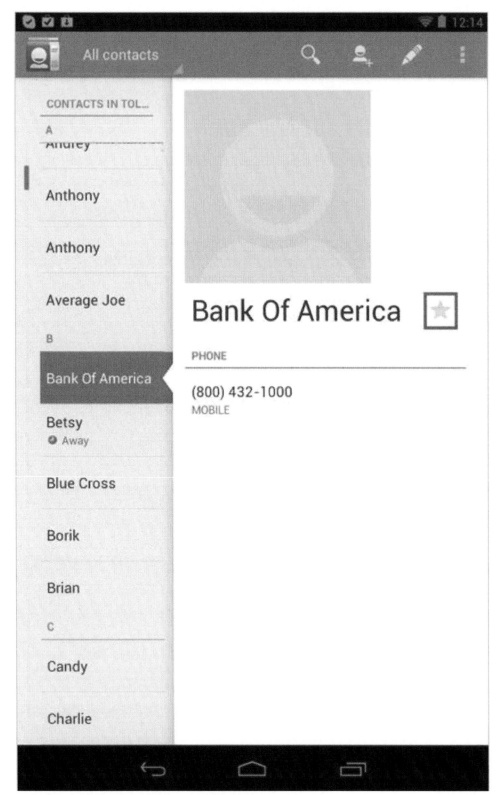

Figure 10: Favorite Icon Outlined

7. Sharing Contact Information via Email

When a contact is stored in the Address Book, all of the information for that contact is available in the form of a Namecard. A Namecard is a VCF file (opened with Outlook or a similar program) that can be shared with others, which conveniently transfers all of the contact's information to other devices. To share contact information:

1. Touch the � icon on the Home screen, or touch the ⬤ icon and then touch the � icon. The Address Book appears.
2. Touch a contact's name. The contact's information appears on the right-hand side of the screen.
3. Touch the blue ☰ icon in the upper right-hand corner of the screen. The Contact menu appears.
4. Touch **Share**. The Sharing Method menu appears, as shown in **Figure 11**.
5. Touch **Gmail**. A new message appears with the Namecard attached, as shown in **Figure 12**.
6. Enter an email address, subject, and optional message by touching each field. The information is entered. Refer to *"Writing an Email"* on page 80 to learn more about composing emails.
7. Touch the ➤ button in the upper right-hand corner of the screen. The email is sent and the contact information is shared. On a mobile device, the recipient can save the Namecard directly to the Address Book, as shown in the iPhone example in **Figure 13**.

Note: Sharing contact information via Bluetooth is not covered in this guide due to its complexity and the fact that devices often fail to communicate with one another properly.

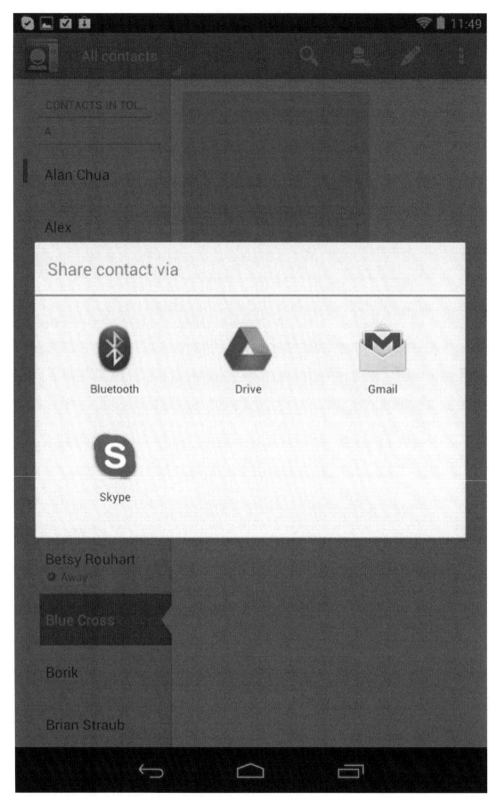

Figure 11: Sharing Method Menu

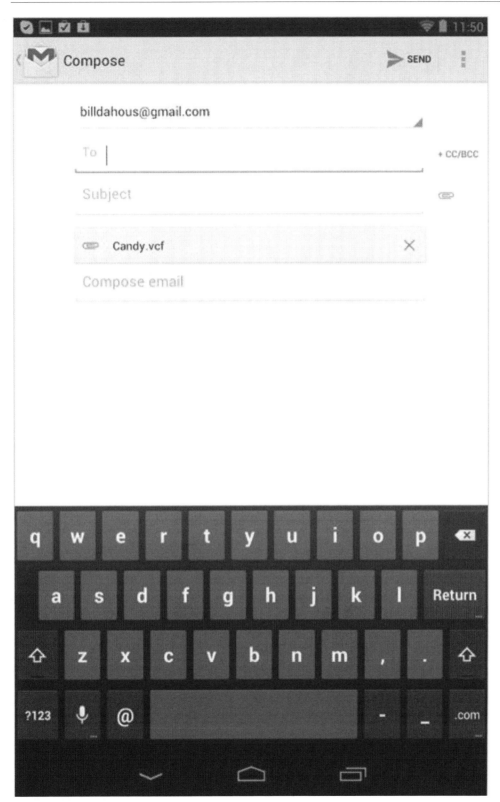

Figure 12: New Message with Attached Namecard

Figure 13: Receiving a Namecard on an iPhone

8. Changing the Way Contacts are Sorted

By default, contacts in the Address Book are sorted alphabetically by first name. For example, John Diss is listed before Ray Beeze because John comes before Ray in the alphabet. The last name is disregarded when sorting, unless there is more than one person with the same first name, in which case it is used to determine which name is listed first. To change the way contacts are sorted:

1. Touch the [icon] icon on the Home screen, or touch the [icon] icon and then touch the [icon] icon. The Address Book appears.

2. Touch the blue [icon] icon in the upper right-hand corner of the screen. The Contact menu appears.

3. Touch **Settings**. The Address Book Settings screen appears, as shown in **Figure 14**.

4. Touch **Sort list by**. The Sorting window appears, as shown in **Figure 15**.

5. Touch **Last name**. The contacts in the Address Book will now be sorted according to their last name. Using the example in this section, Ray Beeze would now come before John Diss.

6. Touch **First name**. The contacts in the Address Book will now be sorted according to their first name.

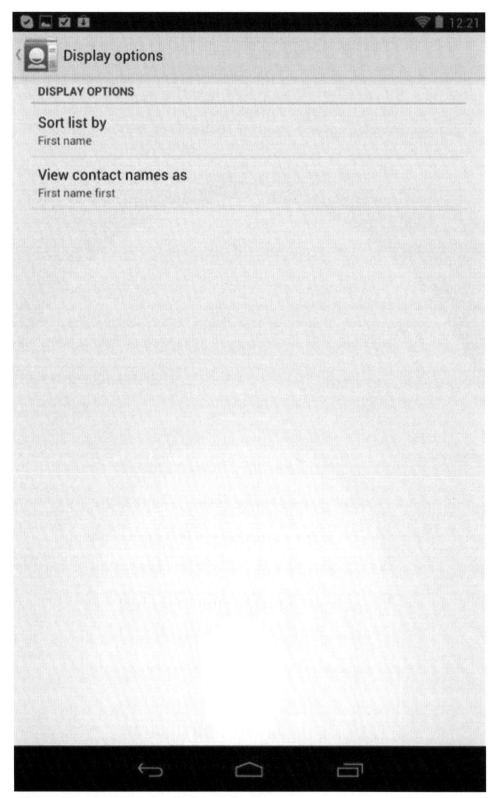

Figure 14: Address Book Settings Screen

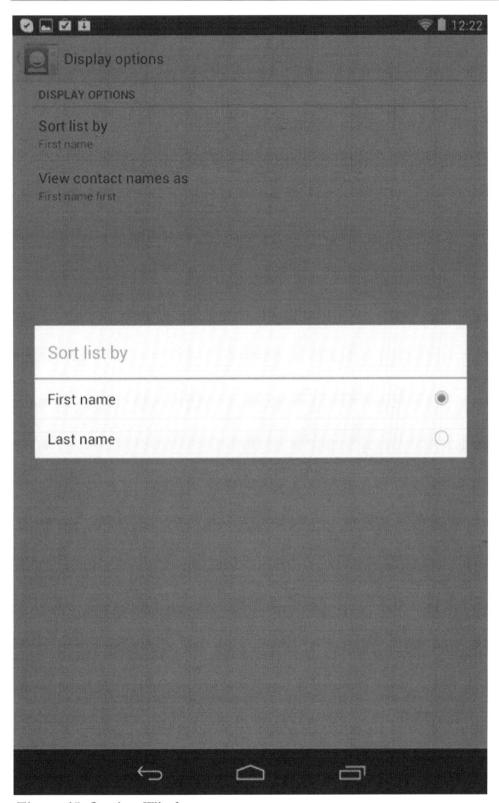

Figure 15: Sorting Window

9. Changing the Way Contacts are Displayed

By default, contacts in the Address Book are displayed with the first name appearing first. For example, Sarah Bellum is displayed as "Sarah Bellum." To change the way contacts are displayed:

1. Touch the ![icon] icon on the Home screen, or touch the ![icon] icon and then touch the ![icon] icon. The Address Book appears.
2. Touch the blue ![icon] icon in the upper right-hand corner of the screen. The Contact menu appears.
3. Touch **Settings**. The Address Book Settings screen appears.
4. Touch **View contact names as**. The Contact Display window appears, as shown in **Figure 16**.
5. Touch **Last name first**. Contacts will now be displayed with the last name appearing first. Using the example in this section, Sarah Bellum will now be displayed as "Bellum, Sarah."
6. Touch **First name first**. Contacts will now be displayed with the first name appearing first.

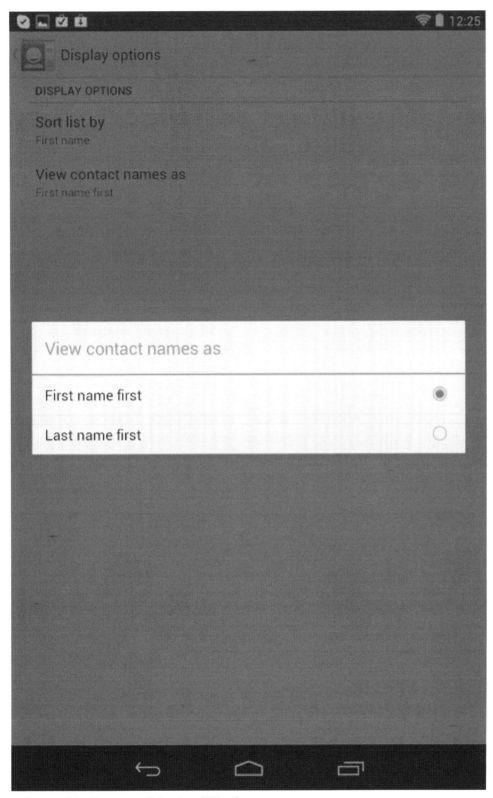

Figure 16: Contact Display Window

Using the Chrome Web Browser

Table of Contents

1. Navigating to a Website

One way to visit a website is to enter its Web address in the address bar. To navigate to a website using its Web address:

1. Touch the icon on the Home screen, or touch the icon and then touch the icon. The Chrome browser opens and a list of the recently visited websites appears, as shown in **Figure 1**.
2. Touch **Search or type URL** in the address bar at the top of the screen, as outlined in **Figure 1**. The Address bar is selected and the keyboard appears.
3. Enter a Web address and touch the **Go** button. Chrome navigates to the website.

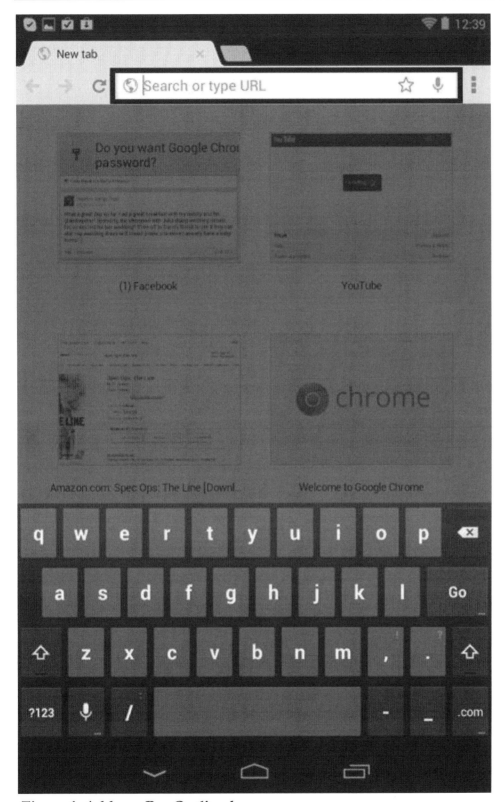

Figure 1: Address Bar Outlined

2. Adding and Viewing Bookmarks

The Nexus 7 can store websites as bookmarks to access them faster. These bookmarks will appear both on your mobile devices and the computers that are logged in to your Google account in the Chrome browser. To add a bookmark:

1. Navigate to a website. Refer to *"Navigating to a Website"* on page 138 to learn how.
2. Touch the ☆ icon in the address bar, as outlined in **Figure 2**. The Bookmark Editing window appears, as shown in **Figure 3**.
3. Enter a name for the bookmark. The name of the bookmark is entered.
4. Touch **Mobile Bookmarks** to select the locations where the bookmark should be saved. A list of available bookmark locations appears, as shown in **Figure 4**.
5. Touch the desired locations in the list. A ✔ mark appears next to each selected location.
6. Touch **OK**. The bookmark is saved to the selected locations and the Bookmark Editing window reappears.
7. Touch **Save**. The Web page is saved to your bookmarks.

To view your bookmarks:

1. Touch the ⁝ icon in the upper right-hand corner of the browser. The Chrome menu appears, as outlined in Figure 5.
2. Touch **Bookmarks**. The Bookmarks screen appears, as shown in **Figure 6**.
3. Touch a bookmark. Chrome navigates to the selected Web page.

Figure 2: Bookmark Icon Outlined

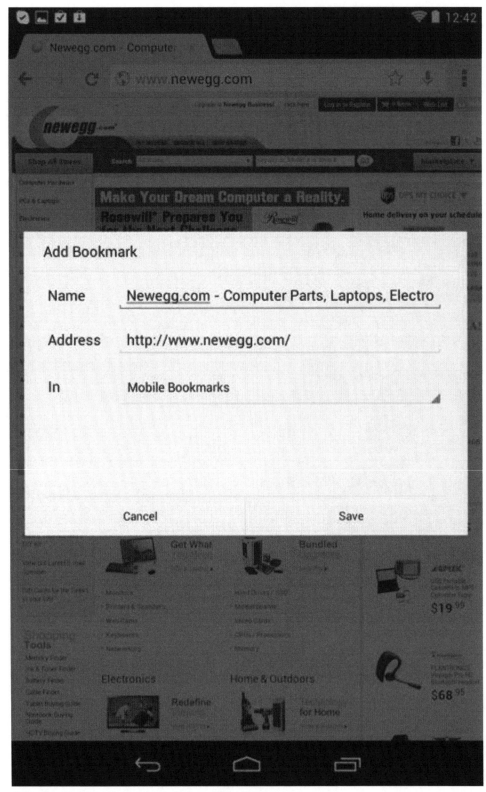

Figure 3: Bookmark Editing Window

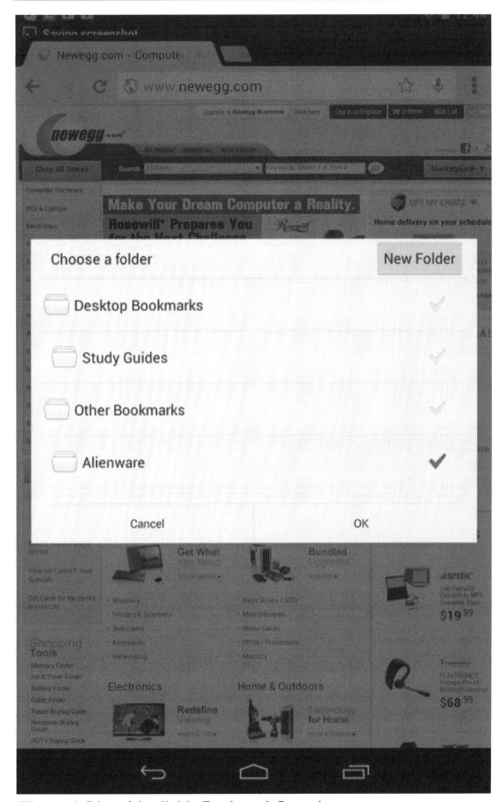

Figure 4: List of Available Bookmark Locations

Figure 5: Chrome Menu

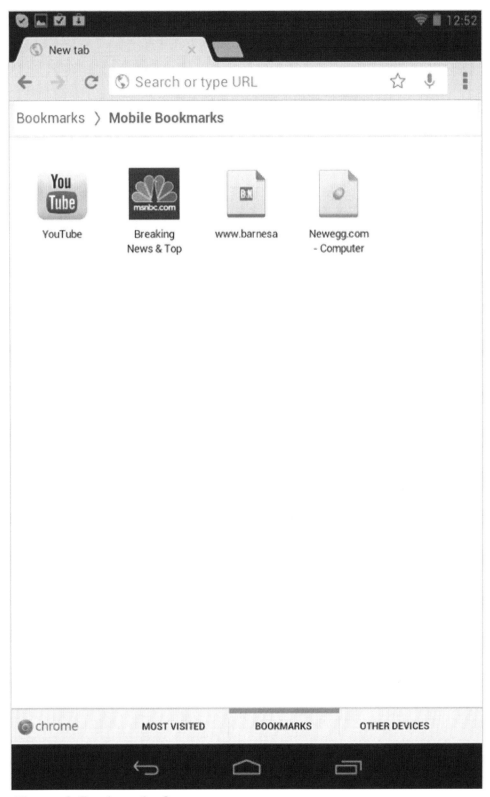

Figure 6: Bookmarks Screen

3. Editing and Deleting Bookmarks

Bookmarks may be edited if a new Web address or label is desired. Bookmarks may also be deleted to free up space.

To edit a bookmark:

1. Touch the ⦙ icon in the upper right-hand corner of the browser. The Chrome menu appears.
2. Touch **Bookmarks**. The Bookmarks screen appears.
3. Touch and hold a bookmark. The Bookmark menu appears, as shown in **Figure 7**.
4. Touch **Edit bookmark**. The Bookmark Editing window appears.
5. Touch a field to change the information. The bookmark is edited.
6. Touch **Save**. The new bookmark information is stored.

To delete a bookmark:

Warning: Once a bookmark is deleted, it is gone for good. There is no confirmation dialog when deleting a bookmark. Make sure that you wish to delete the bookmark before touching Delete Bookmark ***in step 4 below.***

1. Touch the ⦙ icon in the upper right-hand corner of the browser. The Chrome menu appears.
2. Touch **Bookmarks**. The Bookmarks screen appears.
3. Touch and hold a bookmark. The Bookmark menu appears.
4. Touch **Delete bookmark**. The bookmark is deleted.

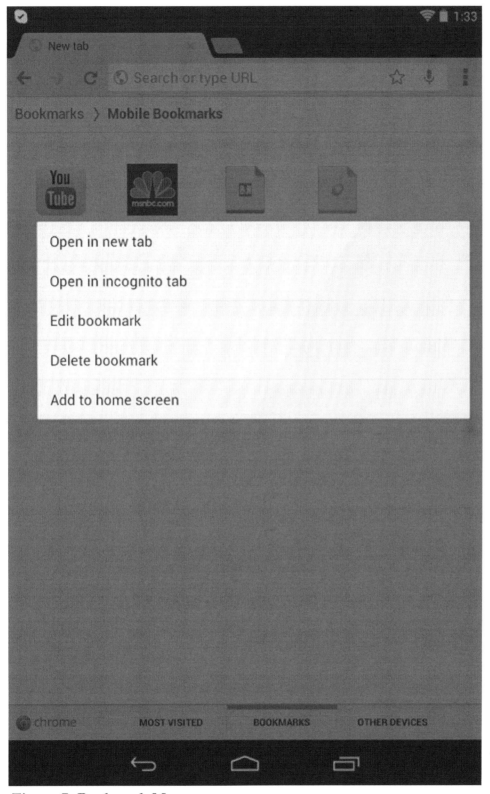

Figure 7: Bookmark Menu

4. Opening More than One Website at a Time

The Chrome browser allows you to have more than one Web page opened at once, using separate tabs. The number of tabs that may be opened simultaneously is unlimited. Use the following tips to manage Chrome tabs:

- To add a tab, touch the ▬ icon, as outlined in **Figure 8**. Touch any of the other open tabs to open the Web page that they contain.

- To close a tab, touch the ✖ icon on the right-hand side of a tab, as outlined in **Figure 8**.

- To move a tab, touch and hold it until the other tabs fade to a darker color, and then drag it to the desired location.

- To reveal other tabs when more than three tabs are open, touch any tab and slide it to the left or right, depending on the location of the hidden tabs.

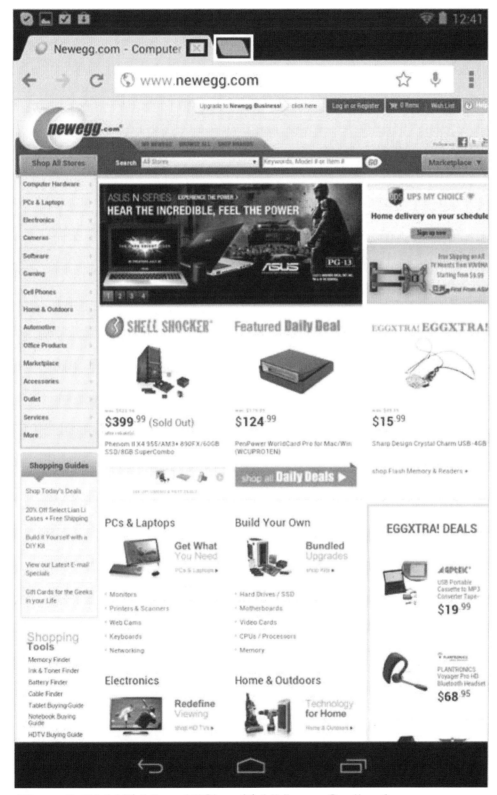

Figure 8: "Add Tab" and "Close Tab" Icons Outlined

5. Link Options

In addition to touching a link to navigate to its destination, there are other Link options. Touch and hold a link to see all Link options, as follow:

- **Open in new tab** - Opens the link in a new tab, so as not lose the current Web page. Refer to *"Opening More than One Website at a Time"* on page 148 to learn how to view other open pages.

- **Open in Incognito tab** - Opens the link in a new Incognito tab, which will prevent you from leaving a trail in the form of a Web History while browsing in the tab.

- **Copy link address** - Copies the Web address to the clipboard.

- **Save link as** - Downloads the Web page to the Nexus 7. The Web page can then be accessed by touching the ⊞ icon and then touching the ⬇ icon. The Nexus 7 does not need to be connected to a Wi-Fi network to access the saved Web page, but it does need an internet connection if you wish to navigate to any of the links on the saved Web page (if applicable).

6. Copying and Pasting Text

Text on any Web page can be selected, copied, and pasted to another location. To copy and paste text:

1. Touch the beginning of the text until a word is highlighted in blue and the ◢ and ◤ markers appear.

2. Touch and drag the ◢ and ◤ markers to select as much text as desired. The Text menu appears at the top of the screen, as outlined in **Figure 9**.
3. Touch **Copy**. The text is copied to the clipboard.
4. To paste the text to another location, such as an application, touch and hold a text field. Touch **Paste**. The text is pasted to the new location.

Note: You can also search the Web using the selected text as the keywords, by touching **Web Search** *in step 3 above.*

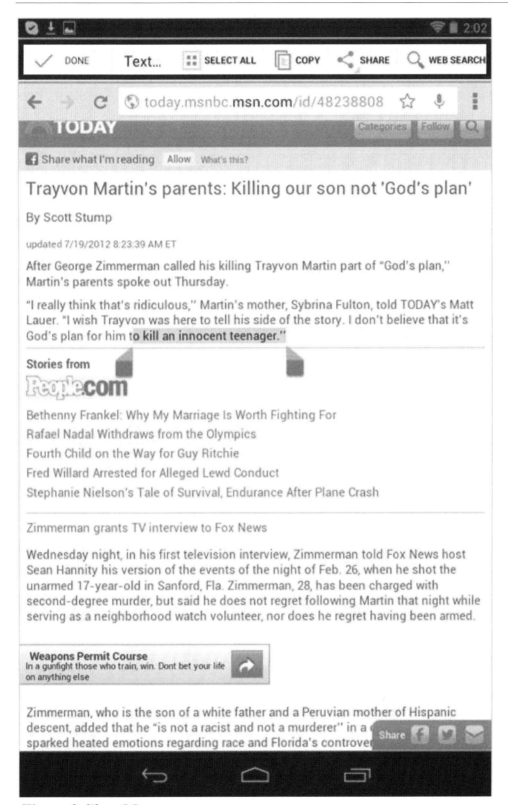

Figure 9: Text Menu

7. Searching a Web Page for a Word or Phrase

While surfing the Web, any Web page can be searched for a word or phrase. To perform a search of a Web page:

1. Touch the ▮ icon in the upper right-hand corner of the screen. The Chrome menu appears.
2. Touch **Find in page**. The 'Find in page' field appears at the top of the screen, as outlined in **Figure 10**.
3. Enter search keywords and touch the [🔍] button. All matching search results are highlighted in yellow on the page, as shown in **Figure 11**.
4. Touch one of the yellow stripes on the right side of the screen, as outlined in **Figure 11**, to navigate to a specific result. The result is highlighted in orange on the page.

Note: You can also touch the ⌃ or ⌄ icons to the right of the Search field to navigate to the previous or next result, respectively.

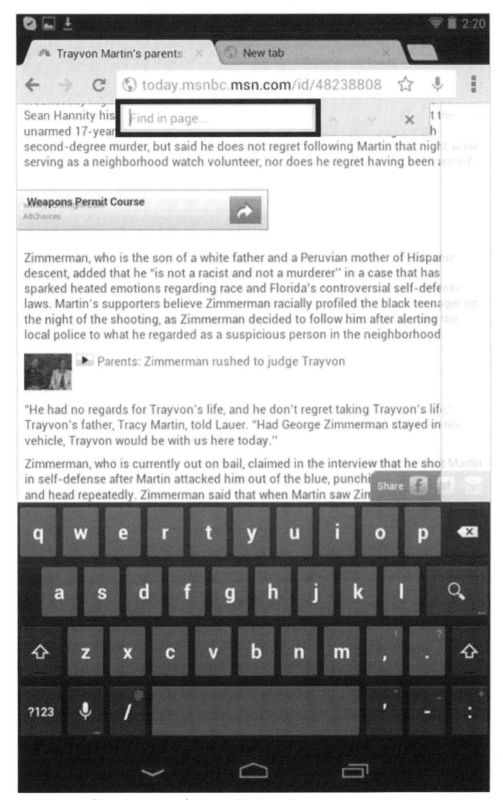

Figure 10: 'Find in Page' Field Outlined

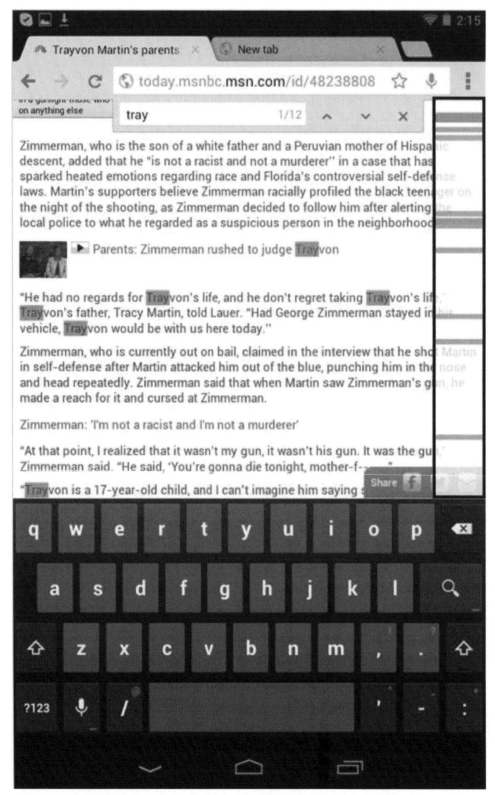

Figure 11: Matching Search Results Highlighted in Yellow

8. Viewing the Most Frequently Visited Websites

The Nexus 7 stores all frequently visited websites. To view the most frequently visited sites:

1. Touch the ⋮ icon in the upper right-hand corner of the browser. The Chrome menu appears.
2. Touch **Bookmarks**. The Bookmarks screen appears.
3. Touch **Most visited** at the bottom of the screen. The most frequently visited sites appear as thumbnails, as shown in **Figure 12**.
4. Touch a site in the list. Chrome navigates to the Web page.

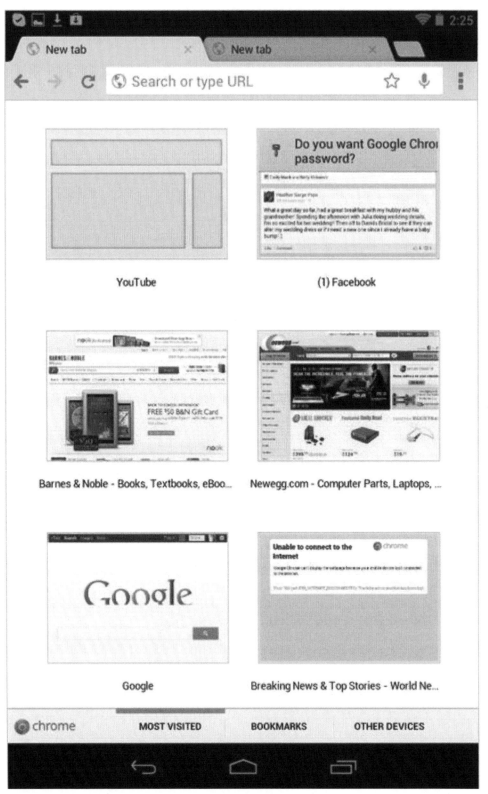

Figure 12: Most Frequently Visited Sites

9. Automatically Filling in Online Forms

Nexus 7's Autofill feature can automatically enter your personal information into online forms by using a predefined Autofill profile. To add a new Autofill profile:

1. Touch the ⋮ icon in the upper right-hand corner of the browser. The Chrome menu appears.
2. Touch **Settings**. The Chrome Settings screen appears, as shown in **Figure 13**.
3. Touch **Autofill forms**. The Autofill Profiles screen appears, as shown in **Figure 14**.
4. Touch **Add profile** under 'Autofill Profiles'. The Add Profile screen appears, as shown in **Figure 15**.
5. Touch each field to enter the associated information. The information is entered.
6. Touch the key at the bottom of the screen. The keyboard is hidden.
7. Touch **Save**. The Autofill profile is saved and the information that you provided will be automatically entered into online forms.

Note: Refer to "Clearing the Data that is Used to Speed Up Browsing" *on page 170 to learn how to delete all saved forms.*

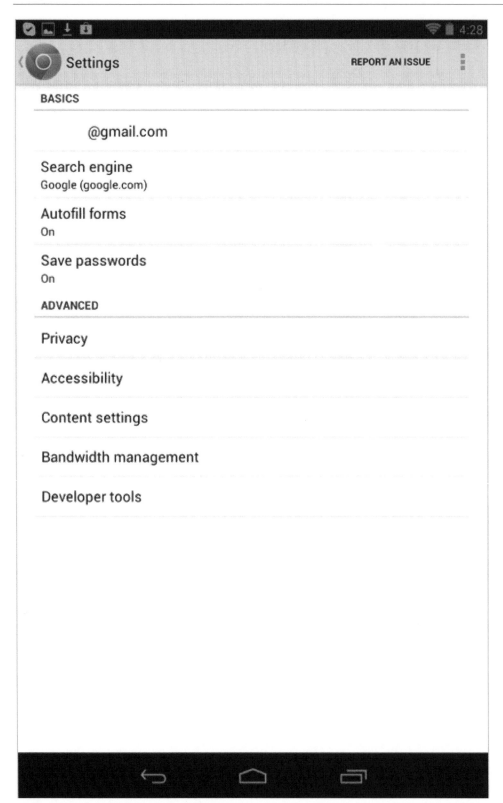

Figure 13: Chrome Settings Screen

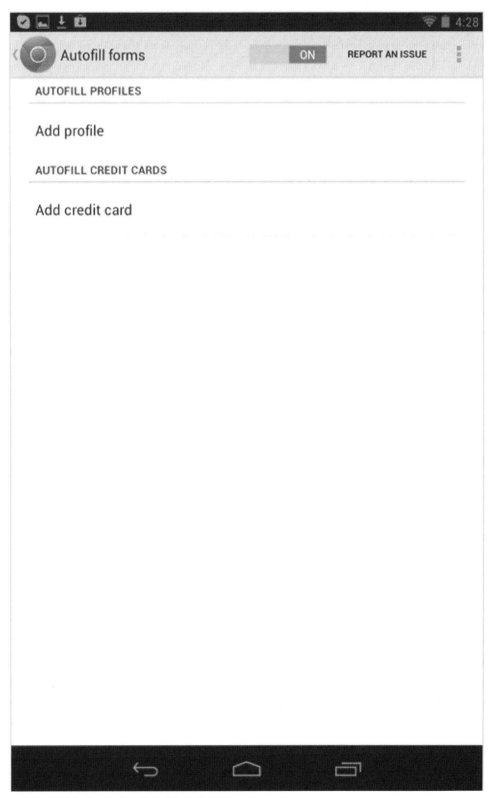

Figure 14: Autofill Profiles Screen

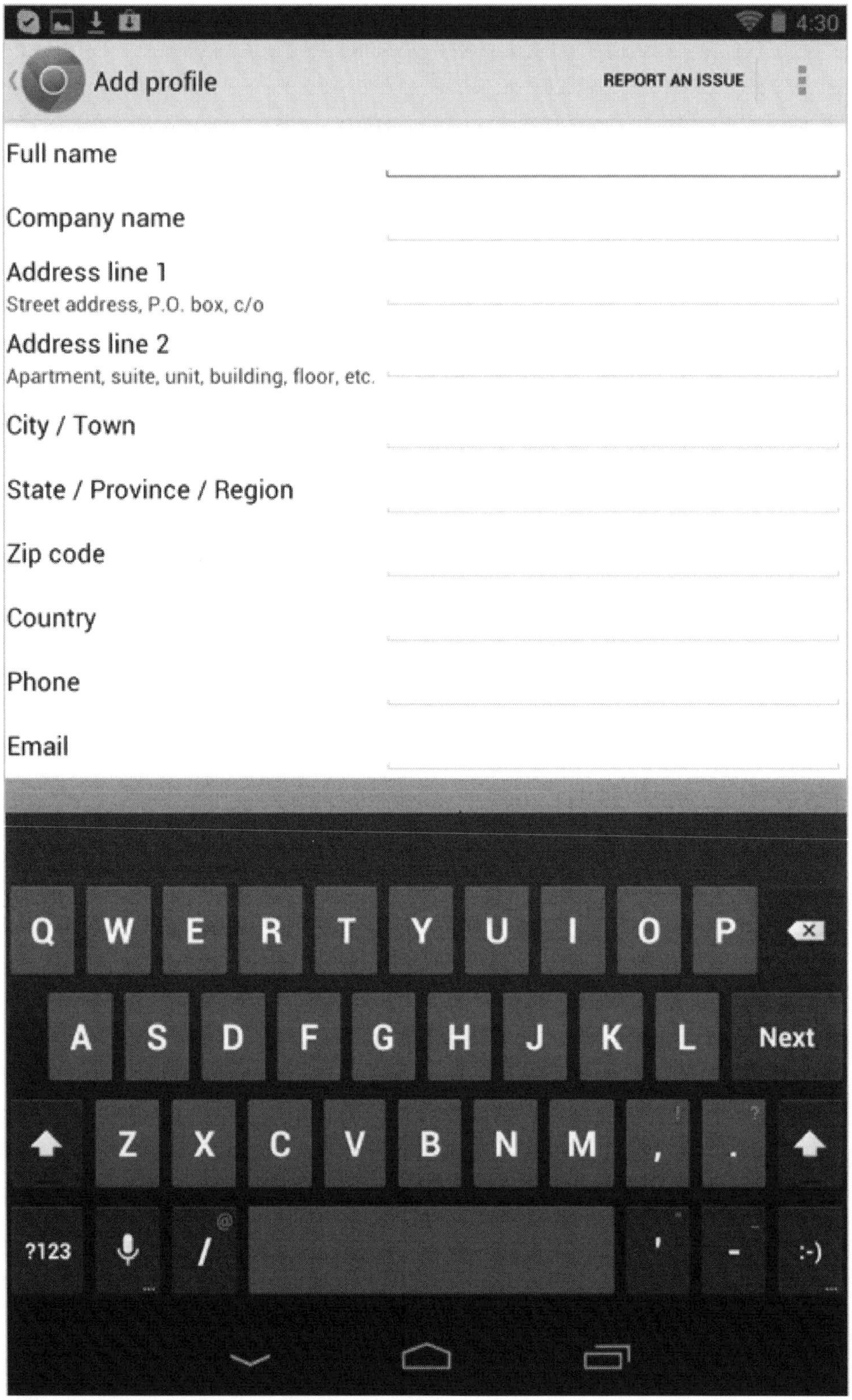

Figure 15: Add Profile Screen

10. Saving and Managing Passwords for Websites

The Chrome browser can save your account credentials for various websites, such as email clients and shopping sites. By default, Chrome offers to save a password when you enter it. In order to protect your privacy, you may also delete saved passwords for specific websites after they have been stored.

To enable the saving of usernames and passwords:

1. Touch the ⣀ icon in the upper right-hand corner of the browser. The Chrome menu appears.
2. Touch **Settings**. The Chrome Settings screen appears.
3. Touch **Save passwords**. The Saved Passwords screen appears, as shown in **Figure 16**.
4. Touch the ⟨ON⟩ switch at the top of the screen, as outlined in **Figure 16**. The ⟨OFF⟩ switch appears and Chrome will no longer offer to save passwords.
5. Touch the ⟨OFF⟩ switch. The ⟨ON⟩ switch appears and Chrome will offer to save passwords every time you enter one.

To delete a stored password for a specific website:

1. Follow steps 1-3 above. The Saved Passwords screen appears.
2. Touch a website under 'Saved Passwords'. The Saved Password URL and email to which the account is assigned appear, as shown in **Figure 17**.
3. Touch **Delete**. The saved password for the website is deleted,

Note: Refer to "Clearing the Data that is Used to Speed Up Browsing" *on page 170 to learn how to delete all saved passwords at once.*

Figure 16: Saved Passwords Screen

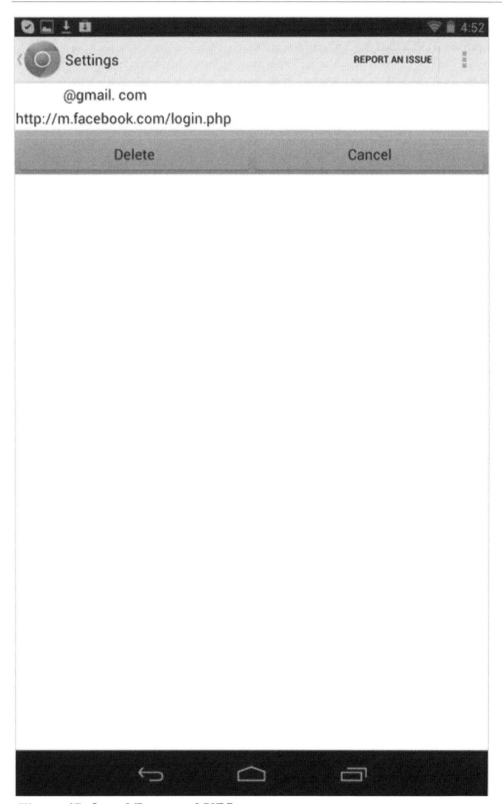

Figure 17: Saved Password URL

11. Setting the Search Engine

Google, Yahoo, or Bing may be used as the default search engine in the Chrome browser. To perform a search at any time, enter a search term in the address bar. Refer to *"Navigating to a Website"* on page 138 to locate the address bar. To set the search engine:

1. Touch the ⋮ icon in the upper right-hand corner of the browser. The Chrome menu appears.
2. Touch **Settings**. The Chrome Settings screen appears.
3. Touch **Search engine**. A list of available search engines appears.
4. Touch a search engine. The search engine is selected and will be used whenever a search is performed.

12. Setting the Font Size

The text size used in the Chrome browser can be changed. To set the browser's font size:

1. Touch the ⋮ icon in the upper right-hand corner of the browser. The Chrome menu appears.
2. Touch **Settings**. The Chrome Settings screen appears.
3. Touch **Accessibility**. The Accessibility Settings screen appears, as shown in **Figure 18**.

4. Touch the ⬤ slider and drag it to the left or right to decrease or increase the font size, respectively. The font size is adjusted and will be used on all websites.

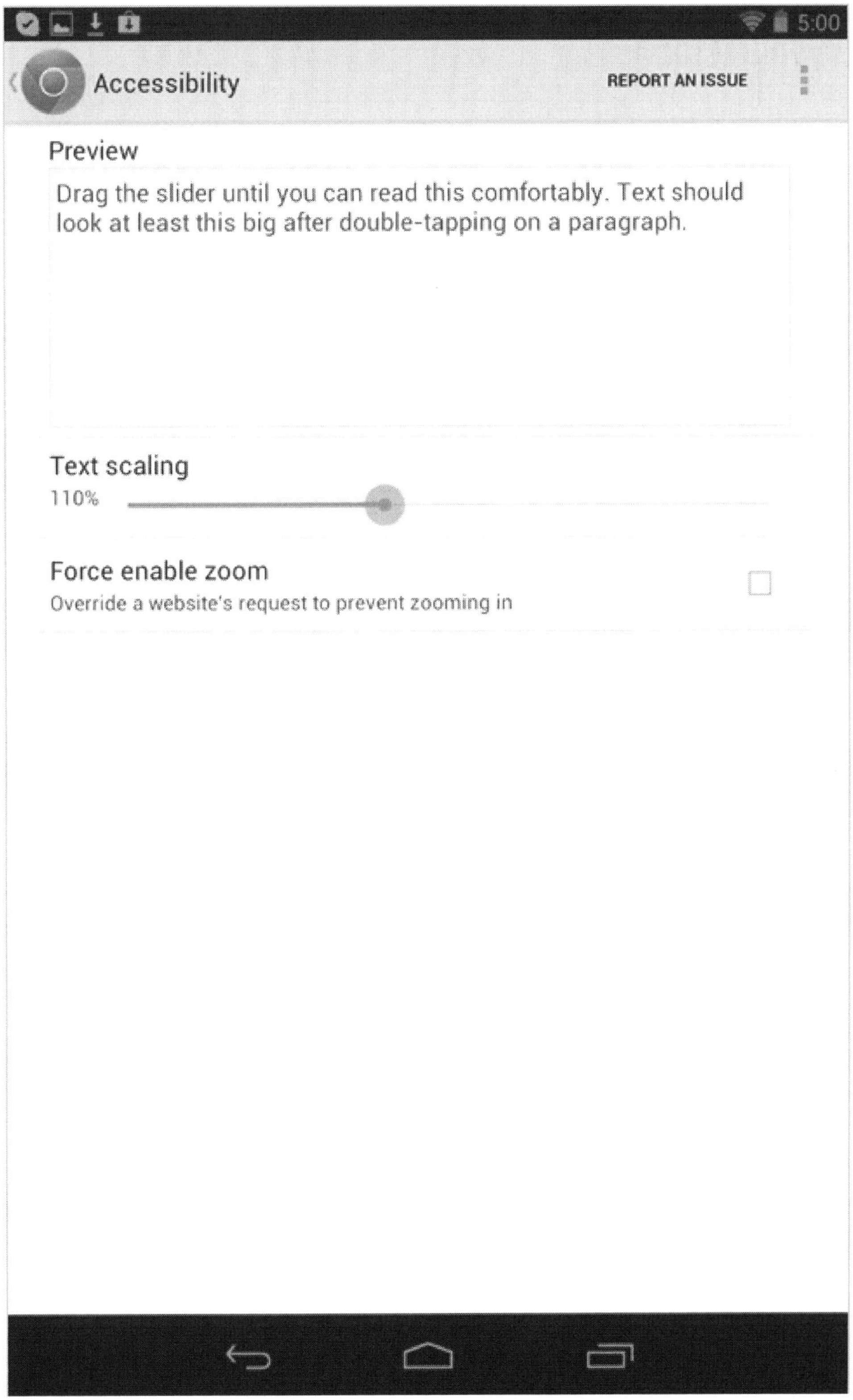

Figure 18: Accessibility Settings Screen

13. Blocking Pop-Up Windows

Some websites may cause pop-up windows to appear, interfering with your surfing. To prevent pop-up windows:

1. Touch the ⋮ icon in the upper right-hand corner of the browser. The Chrome menu appears.
2. Touch **Settings**. The Chrome Settings screen appears.
3. Touch **Content settings**. The Content Settings screen appears, as shown in **Figure 19**.
4. Touch **Block pop-ups**. A ✓ mark appears and Chrome will block pop-up windows.
5. Touch **Block pop-ups** again. The ✓ mark disappears and Chrome will allow pop-up windows.

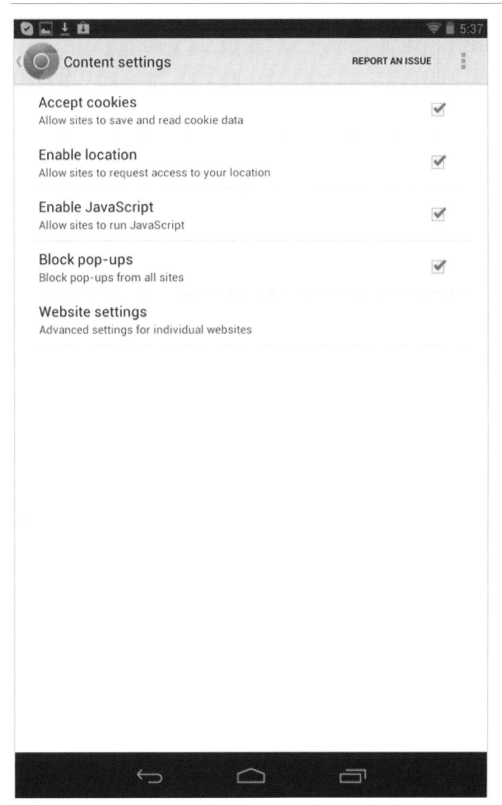

Figure 19: Content Settings Screen

14. Recalling Sites More Quickly on Subsequent Visits

The Chrome browser can store data that is used to quickly recall sites that you have previously visited. This feature provides convenience, but may also take up some space on your device. By default, the Chrome browser stores these data. To recall sites faster on subsequent visits:

1. Touch the ▦ icon in the upper right-hand corner of the browser. The Chrome menu appears.
2. Touch **Settings**. The Chrome Settings screen appears.
3. Touch **Content settings**. The Content Settings screen appears.
4. Touch **Accept cookies**. The ✓ mark disappears and Chrome will not store data that will help to recall sites faster on subsequent visits.
5. Touch **Accept cookies** again. The ✓ mark appears and Chrome will save data that will help to recall sites faster on subsequent visits.

Note: Refer to "Clearing the Data that is Used to Speed Up Browsing" *on page 170 to learn how to delete the data that is used to recall sites faster.*

15. Turning JavaScript On or Off

JavaScript is used primarily for animation and interactive elements on websites, as with games, audio, and video. Turning on JavaScript will allow you to view such content, but may slow down the loading process when you visit sites that contain it. By default, JavaScript is turned on. To turn JavaScript on or off:

1. Touch the ▦ icon in the upper right-hand corner of the browser. The Chrome menu appears.
2. Touch **Settings**. The Chrome Settings screen appears.
3. Touch **Content settings**. The Content Settings screen appears.
4. Touch **Enable JavaScript**. The ✓ mark appears and JavaScript is turned on.
5. Touch **Enable JavaScript** again. The ✓ mark disappears and JavaScript is turned off.

16. Allowing Sites to Request Your Location

Some sites, such as Google, may request your location in order to provide extra services. By default, sites are allowed to request your location. To turn location requests on or off:

1. Touch the ⋮ icon in the upper right-hand corner of the browser. The Chrome menu appears.
2. Touch **Settings**. The Chrome Settings screen appears.
3. Touch **Content settings**. The Content Settings screen appears.
4. Touch **Enable location**. The ✓ mark appears and sites will be allowed to request your location.
5. Touch **Enable location** again. The ✓ mark disappears and sites will be prohibited from requesting your location.

17. Clearing the Data that is Used to Speed Up Browsing

Chrome stores data, which allows it to load previously visited websites and fill in forms more quickly. In order to protect your privacy, you may wish to delete these data. To clear some or all of the data that is used to speed up browsing:

1. Touch the ⦂ icon in the upper right-hand corner of the browser. The Chrome menu appears.
2. Touch **Settings**. The Chrome Settings screen appears.
3. Touch **Privacy**. The Privacy Settings screen appears, as shown in **Figure 20**.
4. Touch **Clear Browsing Data** at the top of the screen, as outlined in **Figure 20**. A list of browsing data types appears, as shown in **Figure 21**.
5. Touch one of the following options to select the type of data for deletion:

- **Clear browsing history** - Deletes all history files, including the addresses of recently visited websites.

- **Clear the cache** - Deletes all Web page data, such as images and other files that comprise a website.

- **Clear cookies, site data** - Deletes all text data, such as site preferences, authentication, or shopping cart contents.

- **Clear saved passwords** - Deletes all stored passwords for various websites, such as email clients, marketplaces, and banking sites.

- **Clear autofill data** - Deletes all form data, including screen names, addresses, phone numbers, and more.

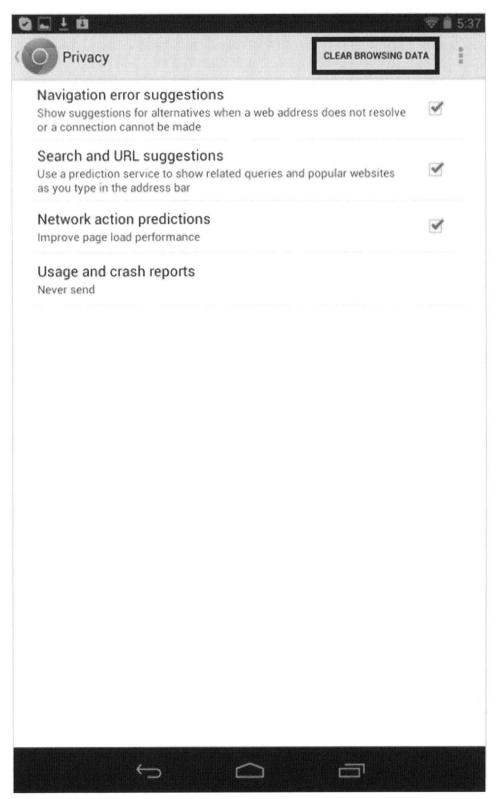

Figure 20: Privacy Settings Screen

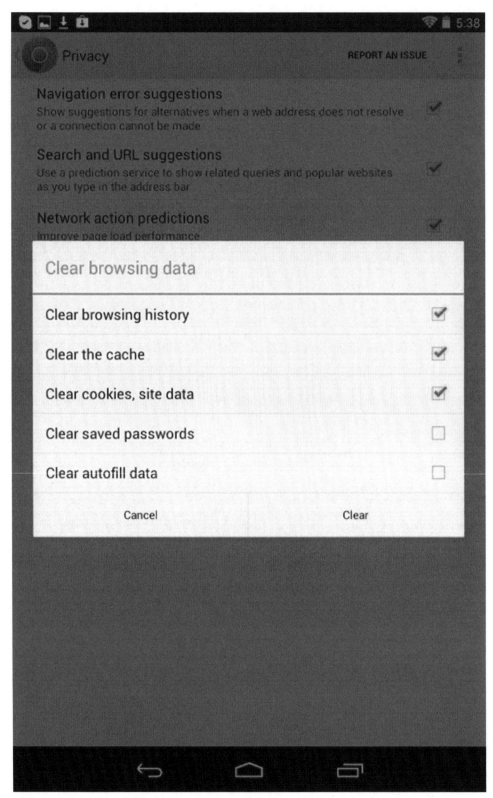

Figure 21: List of Browsing Data Types

18. Turning Suggestions for Searches and Web Addresses On or Off

While you enter a Web address or search query in the address bar, Chrome can automatically make suggestions based on popular choices. To set Chrome to show suggestions when you enter a search query:

1. Touch the ▤ icon in the upper right-hand corner of the browser. The Chrome menu appears.
2. Touch **Settings**. The Chrome Settings screen appears.
3. Touch **Privacy**. The Privacy Settings screen appears.
4. Touch **Search and URL suggestions**. The ✔ mark appears and Chrome will make suggestions when you perform a search or enter a Web address.
5. Touch **Search and URL suggestions** again. The ✔ mark disappears and Chrome will not make suggestions for searches and Web addresses.

Using the Kindle Reader for the Nexus 7

Table of Contents

1. Installing and Running the Kindle Reader for the Nexus 7

The Kindle Reader is an application for reading eBooks purchased from Amazon and other websites in PRC format. The Kindle reader is a free application.

To install the Kindle reader on the Nexus 7:

1. Touch the 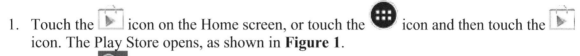 icon on the Home screen, or touch the ⊕ icon and then touch the ▶ icon. The Play Store opens, as shown in **Figure 1**.
2. Touch the 🔍 icon at the top of the screen. The Search field and the keyboard appear.
3. Enter **Kindle** and touch the ⬅ key. A list of search results appears.
4. Touch **Kindle**. The Kindle description appears.
5. Touch the ▮Install▮ button. The Permissions window appears, as shown in **Figure 2**.

6. Touch the ▮Accept & download▮ button. The Kindle application is downloaded and installed.
7. Touch the 📕 icon on the Home screen, or touch the ⊕ icon and then touch the 📕 icon. The Kindle application opens and the Kindle Registration screen appears, as shown in **Figure 3**. If the Welcome screen looks different, then you have downloaded the wrong application.

Note: The Kindle application is free, so do not fall for paid mimics.

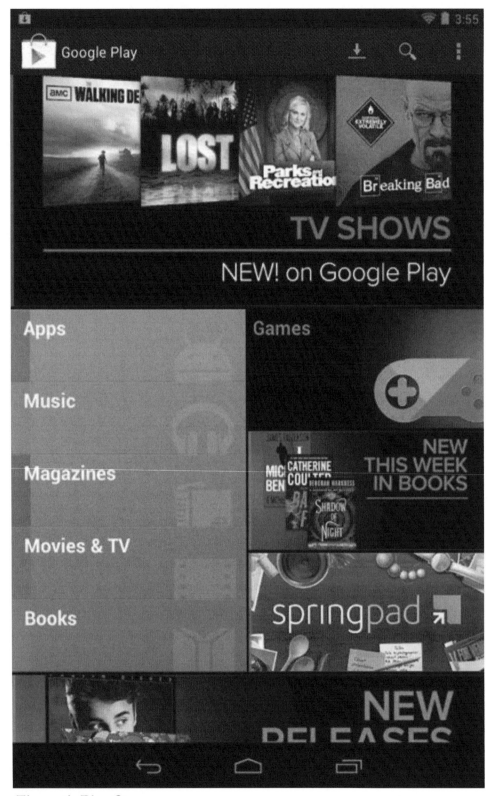

Figure 1: Play Store

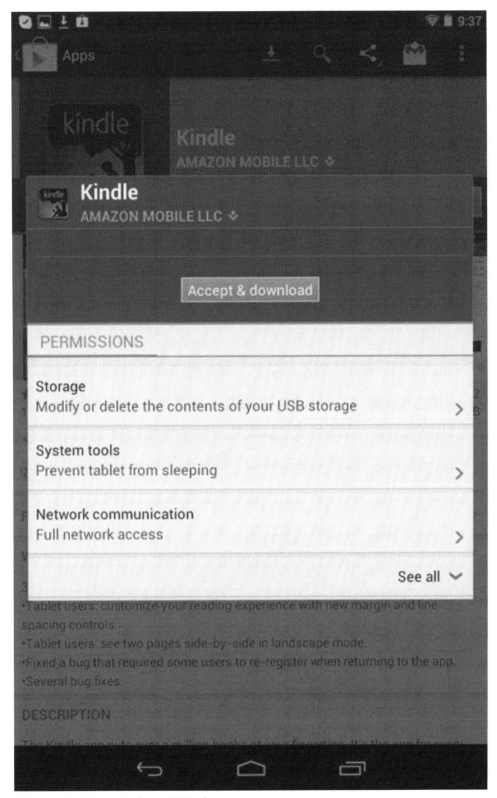

Figure 2: Permissions Window

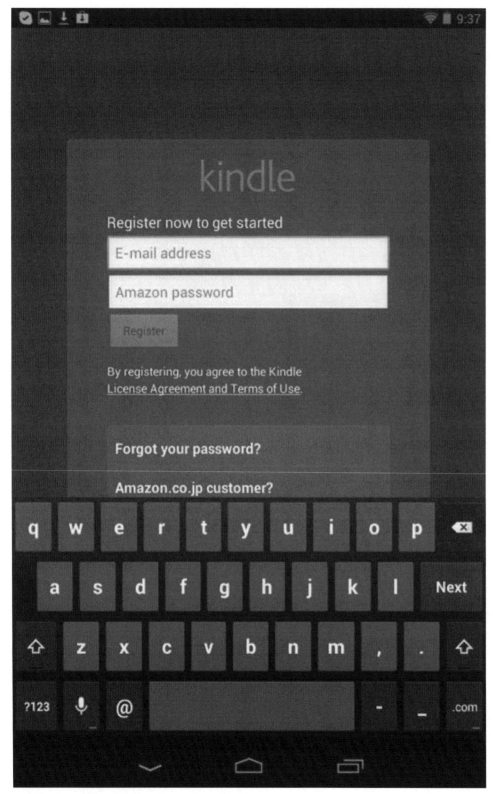

Figure 3: Kindle Registration Screen

2. Buying eBooks (Kindle Reader for the Nexus 7)

The Kindle application for the Nexus 7 allows the purchasing of eBooks directly from the device. To buy an eBook:

1. Touch the ![icon] icon on the Home screen, or touch the ![icon] icon and then touch the ![icon] icon. The Kindle application opens.
2. Touch **Kindle Store** at the top of the screen. The Amazon Kindle storefront appears, as shown in **Figure 4**.
3. Touch the Search field next to 'Kindle Store', as outlined in **Figure 4**. The virtual keyboard appears.
4. Type the name of an eBook or author and touch the ![Go] button. A list of matching results appears. Alternatively, touch a category on the left-hand side of the screen to browse eBooks.
5. Touch the title of an eBook. The eBook description appears, as shown in **Figure 5**.
6. Touch one of the following options on the Description page to perform the corresponding action:

Warning: After touching 'Buy Now with 1-Click', as described below, the eBook is purchased without a confirmation dialog. Make sure that you wish to purchase the eBook before touching 'Buy Now with 1-Click'.

- ![Buy Now with 1-Click®] - The eBook is immediately purchased without a confirmation screen and will appear in the Kindle library on your Nexus 7 momentarily.

Note: If this is your first time purchasing an eBook, the Kindle store will ask for your Amazon email and password. Enter the information and touch **Sign In** *to download the eBook. Touch* **Remember** *after entering the password to avoid having to enter it again in the future. Touch* **Continue** *on the next screen.*

- ![Send sample now] - A short sample of the eBook is downloaded, which is usually limited to the first 5% of the text.

- **Show More** (as outlined in **Figure 6**)- The complete eBook description appears, including customer reviews and product details. This option is not available if the description is small enough to be displayed in its entirety.

Figure 4: Amazon Kindle Storefront

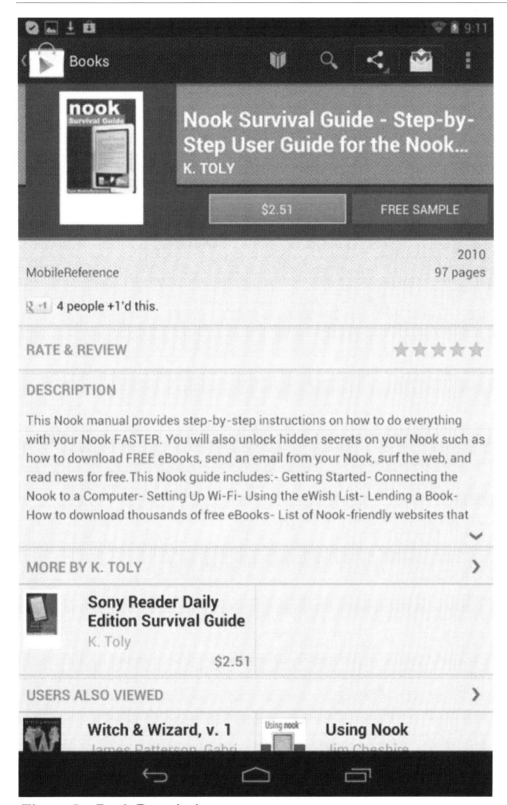

Figure 5: eBook Description

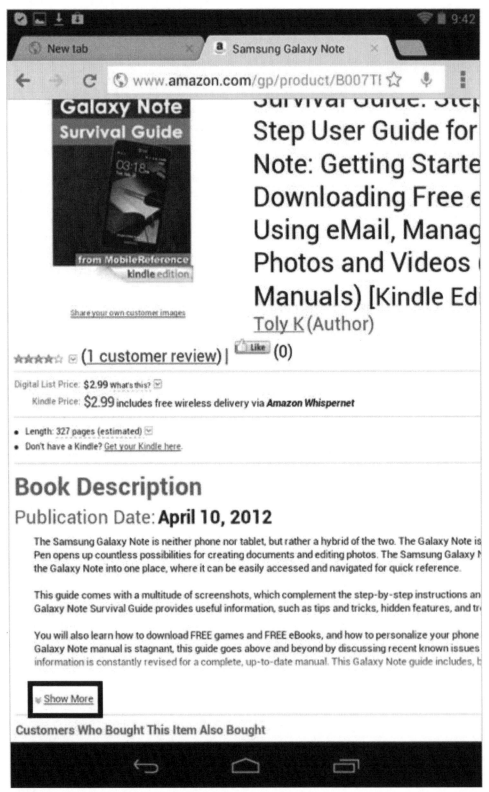

Figure 6: 'Show More' Outlined

3. Finding Free eBooks (Kindle Reader for the Nexus 7)

Amazon has released a number of public domain eBooks free of charge. To view a complete list of free eBooks published by Amazon, search for "Public Domain Books." However, be aware that many of these eBooks were automatically scanned and have never been corrected by a human. As a result, some eBooks have a number of scanning and formatting errors and may be missing complete sections.

4. What Sets MobileReference eBooks Apart?

The quality of Kindle eBooks varies greatly between publishers. Here at MobileReference, we only publish eBooks that are carefully checked for accuracy and completeness by a team of experts.

Looking for a poem or a story in an eBook that contains hundreds of stories is greatly aided by an Active Table of Contents. An Active Table of Contents provides quick access to an eBook's contents via clickable links. Automatically scanned eBooks lack an Active Table of Contents and links to footnotes. MobileReference editors carefully examine each eBook and insert links to individual stories, poems, letters, and footnotes to improve the reading experience and simplify eBook navigation. The results are high quality eBooks with Active Tables of Contents. **Figure 7** shows how the Active Table of Contents appears on the Nexus 7:

WORKS OF ARTHUR CONAN DOYLE. (200+ WORKS) THE COMPLET...

Works of Arthur Conan Doyle from MobileReference

List of Works by Genre and Title
List of Works in Alphabetical Order
List of Works in Chronological Order
Arthur Conan Doyle Biography
About and Navigation

List of Works by Genre and Title

The Complete Collection of Sherlock Holmes :: The Napoleonic Tales :: The Professor Challenger Works :: Other Novels :: Other Short Stories and Collections :: Poetry :: Spiritualist Works :: Works on Current Affairs :: Literary Criticism

The Complete Collection of Sherlock Holmes

A Study in Scarlet
The Sign of Four
The Adventures of Sherlock Holmes

Figure 7: Active Table of Contents

MobileReference pioneered the publication of collections of works by a particular author in a single eBook. This was motivated in part by the desire to reduce the clutter of titles in the digital library. Consider the collection 'Works of Charles Dickens' that contains over 200 works. When purchased individually, each eBook has an entry in your digital library (analogous to the spine of a paper book). To select an eBook in a digital library of 200 eBooks, one needs to scroll through as many as 20 pages of the library (when 10 books are presented on each page). MobileReference's author-collections organize all of these eBooks into one electronic volume that has a single representation in the digital library: 'Works of Charles Dickens'.

Inside author-collections, MobileReference editors diligently index the eBooks alphabetically, chronologically, and by category. For example, a reader looking for 'A Christmas Carol' can click 'Fiction'> 'A Christmas Carol'. Alternatively, a reader can click 'List of works in alphabetical order' > 'C' > 'Christmas Carol'. If a reader forgets the eBook title but remembers that 'A Christmas Carol' was written by Charles Dickens early in his career, he or she can click on the 'List of works in chronological order' > (1843) 'A Christmas Carol'.

By 2012, MobileReference had developed over two hundred collections by Shakespeare, Jane Austen, Mark Twain, Conan Doyle, Jules Verne, Dickens, Tolstoy, and other authors. If you do not see the eBook you want, please email us at **support@soundtells.com** (MobileReference is an imprint of SoundTells, LLC). MobileReference author-collections cost $4.79 or less.

To search for MobileReference ebooks, enter mobi (short for MobileReference) and a keyword; for example: **mobi Dickens**. Refer to page 319 to read more about MobileReference eBooks.

5. Navigating eBooks

Navigating eBooks using the Kindle Reader for the Nexus 7 is made simple by the use of the touchscreen. Use the following tips to navigate an eBook in the Kindle Reader application:

- To turn the pages, touch the page edges or flick your finger to the right or left.

- Touch the key at any time to return to the Kindle library.

- To switch between Landscape and Portrait views, rotate the device. When in Landscape view, two pages at a time are displayed. Refer to *"Turning Automatic Screen Rotation On or Off"* on page 251 to learn how to disable screen rotation.

- Touch an image twice in quick succession to zoom in on it.

Note: If you are having trouble switching between Landscape and Portrait modes, refer to *"Screen or keyboard does not rotate"* on page 312 to resolve the problem.

6. Deleting and Restoring eBooks (Kindle Reader for the Nexus 7)

eBooks can be deleted from the Nexus 7 and stored on the Amazon servers, where they will not take up space on your device. eBooks that have been deleted from the device can be restored at any time at no extra cost to you.

To delete an eBook from the Kindle Home screen, touch and hold the eBook. The eBook menu appears, as shown in **Figure 8**. Touch **Remove from device**. The eBook is deleted from the device.

To restore an eBook to the Kindle Reader library:

1. Touch **Library** in the upper left-hand corner of the screen, as outlined in **Figure 9**. The Item menu appears, as shown in **Figure 10**.
2. Touch **Archived Items**. The Archived Items appear, as shown in **Figure 11**.
3. Touch an eBook in the list. The eBook is downloaded to the Kindle Reader library.

Note: Touch **Library** *in the upper left-hand corner of the screen, and then touch* **Downloaded Items** *to view all eBooks that are currently stored on your device.*

Figure 8: eBook Menu

Figure 9: 'Library' Outlined

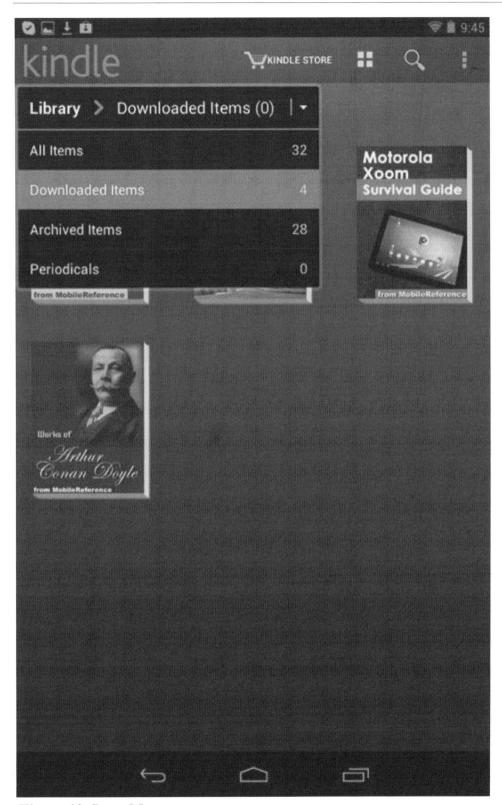

Figure 10: Item Menu

Figure 11: Archived Items

7. Bookmarking a Page

You can bookmark pages in an eBook in order to find them more quickly in the future. To add a bookmark to the current page, touch the upper right-hand corner of the screen. The icon appears in the upper right-hand corner of the page and a bookmark is added. Refer to *"Viewing a List of Your Bookmarks, Notes, and Highlights"* on page 193 to learn how to view a list of all bookmarks in the current eBook.

8. Adding a Note or Highlight

You can highlight a word or phrase and add notes for future reference. To add a note or highlight while reading:

1. Touch and hold a word until the magnifying glass appears. Release the word. The Text menu appears at the top of the screen, as outlined in **Figure 12**.

2. Touch the and markers to the left and right of the word, and drag them to select more text. The text is selected.

3. Touch **Highlight** at the top of the screen and then touch **Done** in the upper left-hand corner of the screen. The word or phrase is highlighted in yellow. Alternatively, touch **Note** at the top of the screen. Enter a note and touch the Save button to add it.

Screen Objects to learn more about accessing applications.

Installing Paid Applications

1. Touch **Buy**. A warning appears regarding the application's access to various parts of the Xoom. Touch **OK** at the bottom left of the screen.

2. Enter your credit card information, which Google Checkout requests the first time you purchase an application. The information is saved. On all subsequent purchases, the screen shown in Figure 8 appears.

3. Touch **OK**. The application is purchased and begins to download. A confirmation appears on the screen when the application has installed.

> **cred·it** /ˈkredit/ *n.* **1** the ability of a customer to obtain goods or services before payment, based on the trust that payment will be made in the future: *I've got unlimited credit.*
>   <SPECIAL USAGE> the money lent or made available under such an arrangement: *the bank*
>
>   **Full Definition**

Figure 12: Text Menu

9. Viewing a List of Your Bookmarks, Notes, and Highlights

To view a list of all bookmarks, notes, and highlights:

1. Touch anywhere on the page. The Kindle options appear at the top of the screen, as outlined in **Figure 13**.

2. Touch the ▓ icon in the upper right-hand corner of the screen, as outlined in **Figure 14**. The eBook options appear, as shown in **Figure 14**.

3. Touch **View My Notes & Marks**. A list of bookmarks, notes, and highlights appears, as shown in **Figure 15**.

4. Touch an item in the list. The Kindle Reader navigates to the corresponding location.

Figure 13: Kindle Options

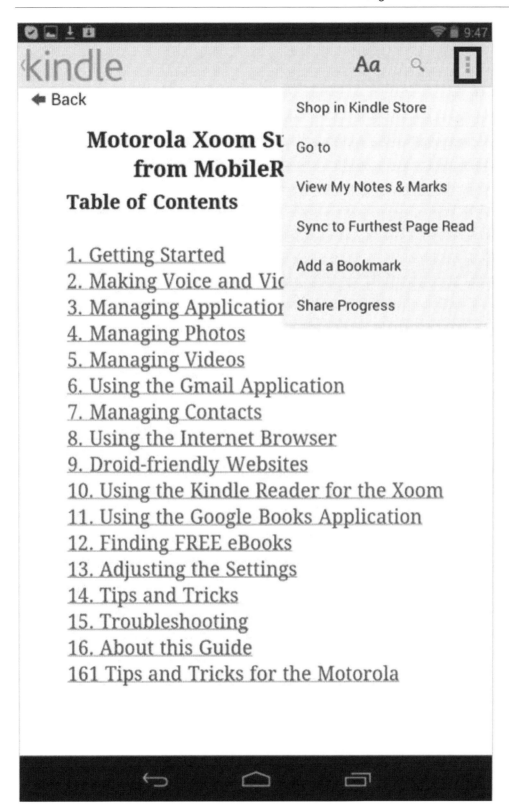

Figure 14: eBook Options

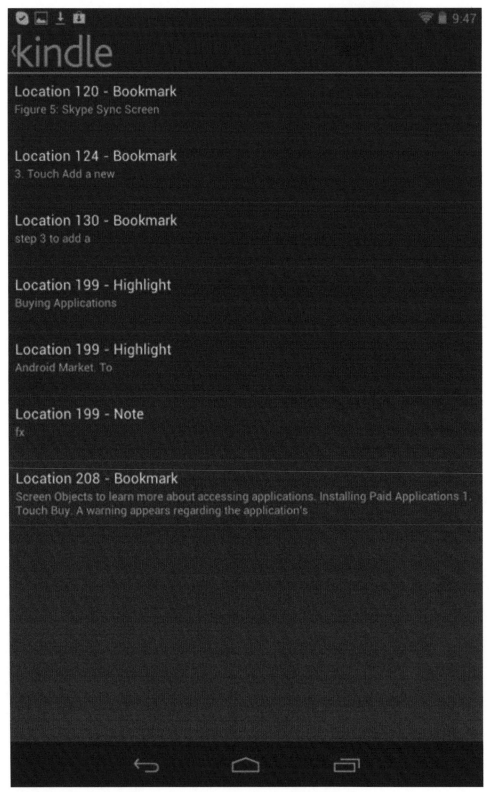

Figure 15: List of Bookmarks, Notes, and Highlights

10. Navigating to a Specific Location

You can navigate to any location in an eBook quickly. To navigate to a specific location in an eBook:

1. Touch anywhere on the page. The Kindle options appear at the top of the screen.
2. Touch the ▓ icon in the upper right-hand corner of the screen.
3. Touch **Go to**. The Go To menu appears, as outlined in **Figure 16**.
4. Touch one of the following options to navigate to the corresponding location:

- **Cover** - Navigates to the cover of the eBook, which is always the first page.

- **Table of Contents** - Navigates to the Table of Contents of the eBook (some eBooks may not have a Table of Contents, in which case this option will be grayed out).

- **Beginning** - Navigates to the beginning of the eBook, which is usually the first page after the cover or the Table of Contents.

- **Page** - Navigates to a specific page, which corresponds to the actual page number in the paperback version of the eBook (not available in all eBooks).

- **Location** - Navigates to a specific location, which can be entered using the keypad in the Enter Location window, as shown in **Figure 17**. Enter a location number and touch the

  Go button. The Kindle Reader navigates to the selected location.

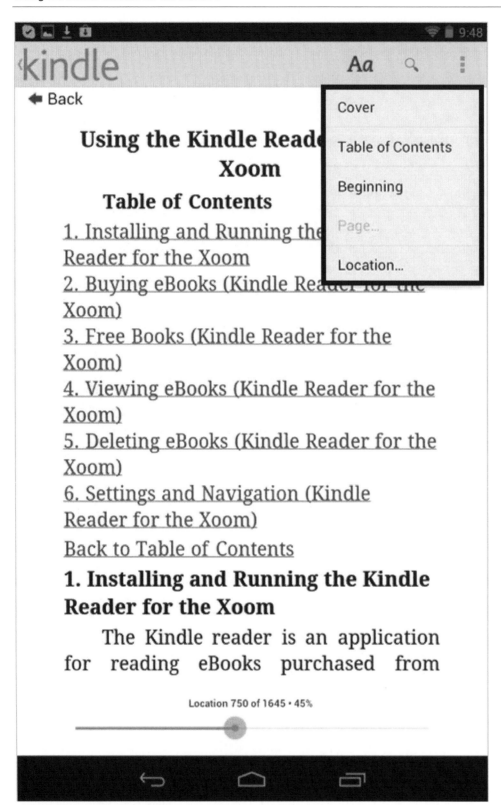

Figure 16: Go To Menu

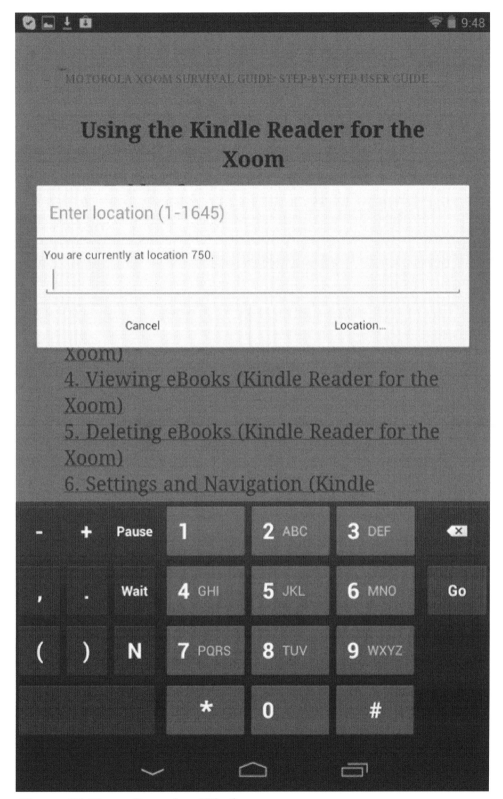

Figure 17: Enter Location Window

11. Adjusting the Font Size

If you have trouble seeing the text, try adjusting the font size. To increase the font size, touch the screen with two fingers close together and move them apart. The font size is increased. To decrease the font size, touch the screen with two fingers spread apart and move them close together. The font size is decreased.

12. Adjusting the Size of the Margins

The amount of white space above, below, and on each side of the main text can be adjusted. To adjust the size of the margins:

1. Touch anywhere on the page. The Kindle options appear at the top of the screen.
2. Touch the Aa icon in the Kindle options. The Page options appear, as shown in **Figure 18**.
3. Touch one of the following icons below 'Margin size' to adjust the margins:

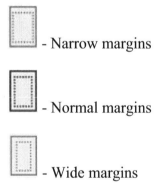 - Narrow margins

- Normal margins

- Wide margins

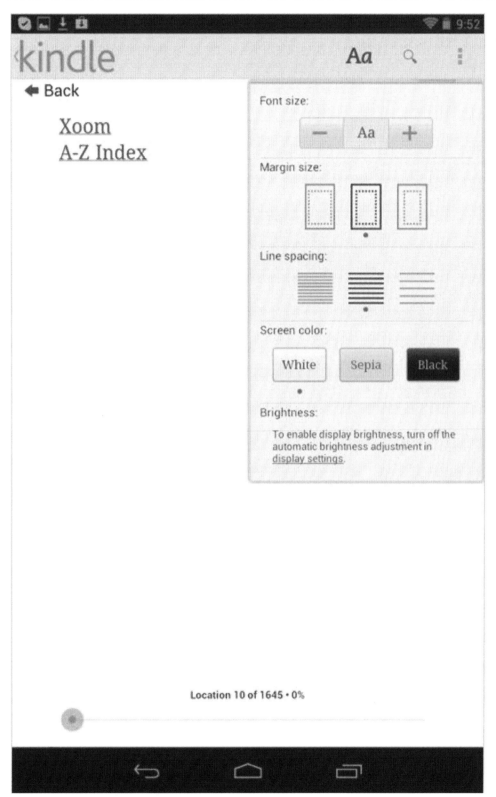

Figure 18: Page Options

13. Adjusting the Line Spacing

In order to provide a more comfortable reading experience, the spacing between the lines of text can be adjusted. To adjust the line spacing:

1. Touch anywhere on the page. The Kindle options appear at the top of the screen.
2. Touch the Aa icon in the Kindle options. The Page options appear.
3. Touch one of the following icons below 'Line spacing' to adjust the line spacing:

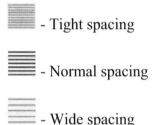 - Tight spacing

- Normal spacing

- Wide spacing

14. Adjusting the Color of the Pages

In order to reduce the strain on your eyes, you may wish to change the color of the pages. To adjust the color of the pages:

1. Touch anywhere on the page. The Kindle options appear at the top of the screen.
2. Touch the Aa icon in the Kindle options. The Page options appear.
3. Touch one of the following icons below 'Screen color' to adjust the color of the pages:

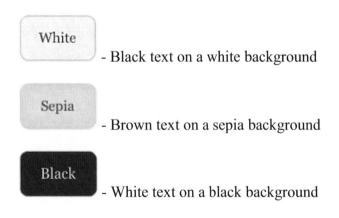

White - Black text on a white background

Sepia - Brown text on a sepia background

Black - White text on a black background

15. Looking Up the Definition of a Word

The Kindle Reader application can display the definition of any word that is contained in the device's dictionary. To define a word:

1. Touch and hold the word that you wish to define. A short definition is displayed at the bottom of the screen, as outlined in **Figure 19**.
2. Touch **Full Definition** at the bottom right-hand corner of the screen. A detailed definition appears, as shown in **Figure 20**.
3. Touch the ⬅️ key. The page where you left off re-appears.

Note: If you do not see a definition, touch the **Download** *button at the bottom of the screen to download a dictionary to the Nexus 7.*

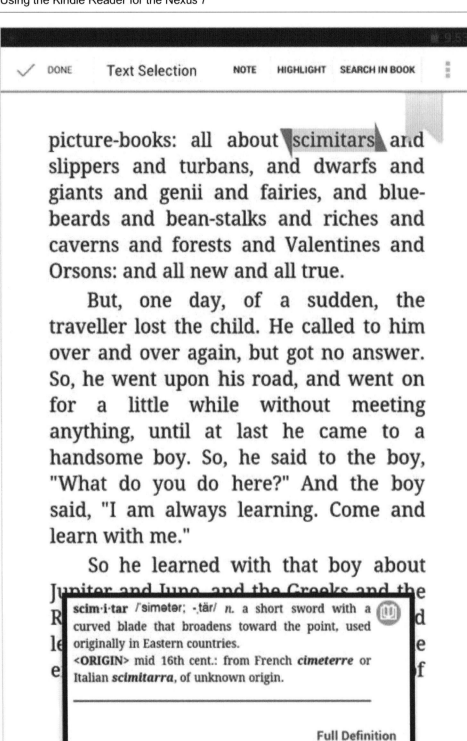

Figure 19: Short Definition

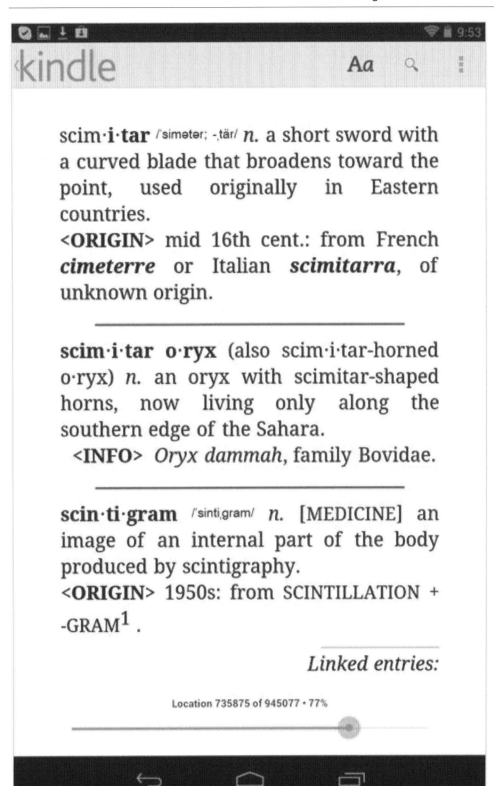

Figure 20: Detailed Definition

Using the Play Books Application for the Nexus 7

Table of Contents

1. Buying eBooks (Play Books for the Nexus 7)

You may purchase eBooks from the Play Books market using the pre-loaded Play Books application. To buy eBooks in Play Books:

1. Touch the ![book icon] icon on the Home screen, or touch the ![apps icon] icon and then touch the ![book icon] icon. The Play Books application opens and the eBook library appears, as shown in **Figure 1**.

2. Touch the ![store icon] icon at the top of the screen, as outlined in **Figure 1**. The Play Store eBook market appears, as shown in **Figure 2**.

3. Touch a category on the left-hand side of the screen, or touch the ![search icon] icon in the upper right-hand corner of the screen to search for an eBook. The Search field appears.

4. Touch the title of an eBook. The eBook description appears, as shown in **Figure 3**.

5. Touch the price of the eBook or touch the **FREE** button if the eBook is free. The eBook Purchase Confirmation dialog appears, as shown in **Figure 4**.

6. Touch the **Accept & buy** button. The eBook is purchased and downloaded to the Nexus 7.

7. Touch the **Open** button. The eBook opens.

Note: If this is your first time purchasing an eBook or application with Google checkout, you will need to enter your credit card number and then touch **Save and continue**.

Figure 1: eBook Library in Play Books

Figure 2: Play Store eBook Market

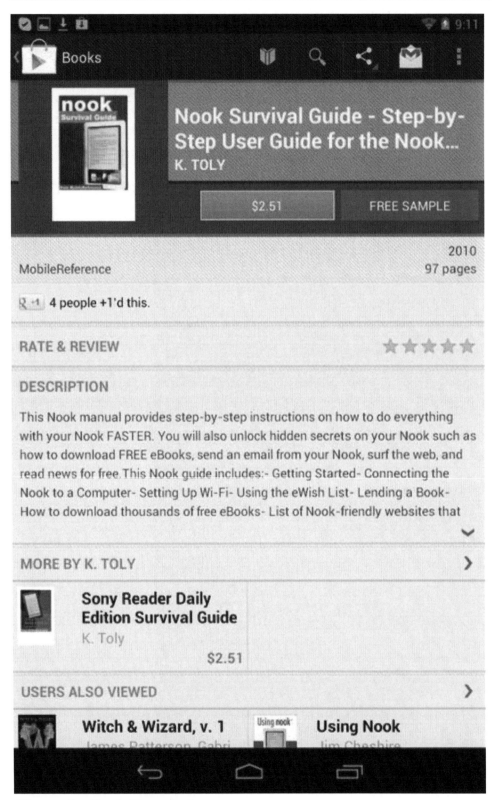

Figure 3: eBook Description

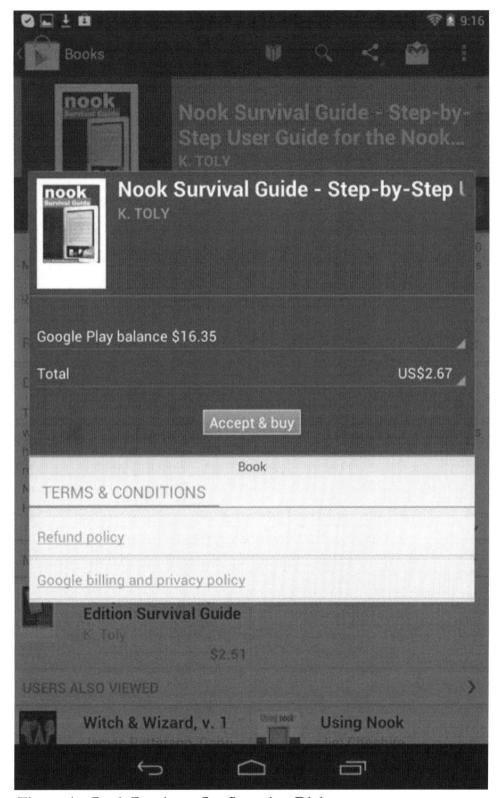

Figure 4: eBook Purchase Confirmation Dialog

2. Reading eBooks (Play Books for the Nexus 7)

Touch an eBook in the Play Books library to open it. Use the following tips to navigate an eBook:

- To turn the pages, touch the page edges or flick your finger to the right or left.

- Touch the key at any time to return to the Play Books library.

- To switch between Landscape and Portrait views, rotate the device. When in Landscape view, two pages at a time are displayed. Refer to *"Turning Automatic Screen Rotation On or Off"* on page 251 to learn how to disable screen rotation.

3. Changing the Color of the Pages (Play Books for the Nexus 7)

In order to reduce the strain on your eyes, you may wish to change the color of the pages. To adjust the color of the pages:

1. Touch the screen anywhere. The eBook Control buttons appear in the upper right-hand corner of the screen, as outlined in **Figure 5**.
2. Touch **Aa** in the upper right-hand corner of the screen. The eBook settings appear at the bottom of the screen, as shown in **Figure 6**.
3. Touch **Day** under 'Theme'. A list of available themes appears, which include 'Day' and 'Night'.
4. Touch **Night**. The page color turns black and the text turns white.
5. Touch **Day**. The page and text color are returned to default, black text on a white background.

Note: Touch anywhere outside of the eBook settings to hide them.

Motorola Xoom Survival

- At the home screen, slide your finger to the left or right to access additional home screens. The Xoom allows you to customize up to eight home screens.

- At the home screen, touch the screen with the thumb and forefinger and bring them together to 'pinch' the screen. All available home screens are shown. Touch a home screen to open it. Touch the ✛ icon to add another home screen.

- Touch the ◀ button at any time to return to the previous screen or menu, or to hide the keyboard.

Back to Top

5. Types of Home Screen Objects

Each home screen on the Xoom is fully customizable. Click Organizing Home Screen Objects to learn how to customize the home screens. Each screen can hold one or more of the following items:

- **Widget** - A tool that can be used directly on the home screen without opening like an application. Widgets usually take up a fraction of the screen, while applications are added as icons. The Books widget is shown in Figure 6.

- **Application** - A program that opens in a new window, such as Gmail or a game. Applications are added to the home screen as icons.

- **Shortcut** - A shortcut to just about anything on your Xoom. Make a shortcut to a settings screen, application, or a set of directions for a single location.

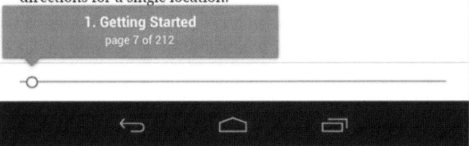

Figure 5: eBook Control Buttons

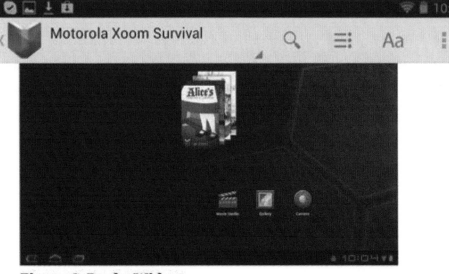

10:58
Motorola Xoom Survival
Aa
Alice's
10:04
Figure 6: Books Widget
Back to Top
6. Organizing Home Screen Objects
Customize the home screen by adding, deleting, or moving objects. Click Types of Home Screen Objects to learn more about objects. To add an object to a home screen:
1. Touch the icon at the top right of the home screen. The Add to Home screen menu appears, as shown in Figure 7.
THEME
Day
BRIGHTNESS
AUTO
TYPEFACE
Default
LINE HEIGHT
TEXT ALIGNMENT
Default
FONT SIZE
T-
T+

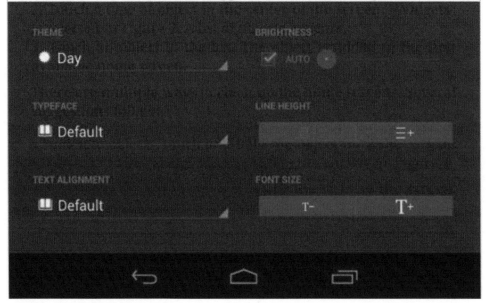

Figure 6: eBook Settings

4. Changing the Font Style

In order to make text more easily readable, you may wish to change the look of the font. The change the font style:

1. Touch the screen anywhere. The eBook Control buttons appear in the upper right-hand corner of the screen.
2. Touch **Aa** in the upper right-hand corner of the screen. The eBook settings appear at the bottom of the screen.
3. Touch **Default** under 'Typeface'. A list of available font styles appears, as shown in **Figure 7**.
4. Touch a font style in the list. The font style is set to your selection.
5. Touch anywhere outside of the eBook settings. The eBook settings are hidden.

desired location. Move the object to the edge of the screen to move it to another home screen.

Figure 7: List of Available Font Styles

5. Changing the Alignment of the Text

Depending on your preference, you may align the text to the left in order to create more white space on the whole, or you may justify the text in order to make the left and right page margins equal in size. To change the alignment of the text:

1. Touch the screen anywhere. The eBook Control buttons appear in the upper right-hand corner of the screen.
2. Touch **Aa** in the upper right-hand corner of the screen. The eBook settings appear at the bottom of the screen.
3. Touch **Default** under 'Text Alignment'. A list of available alignments appears, which are 'Left' and 'Justify'. The 'Default' and 'Justify' settings are equivalent.
4. Touch **Left**. The text is aligned to the left.
5. Touch **Justify**. The text is aligned in such a way so as to lie flat against both the left and right margins, which will create more white space between the words.

6. Adjusting the Line Spacing

In order to provide a more comfortable reading experience, the spacing between the lines of text can be adjusted. To adjust the line spacing:

1. Touch the screen anywhere. The eBook Control buttons appear in the upper right-hand corner of the screen.
2. Touch **Aa** in the upper right-hand corner of the screen. The eBook settings appear at the bottom of the screen.
3. Touch the ▤⁺ button under 'Line Height' to increase the line spacing, or touch the ▤⁻ button to decrease it, as outlined in **Figure 8**. The line spacing is adjusted accordingly.

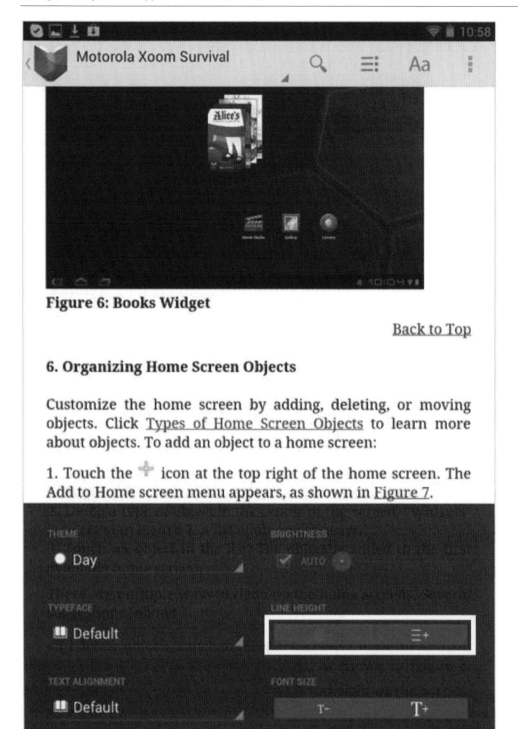

Figure 6: Books Widget

<u>Back to Top</u>

6. Organizing Home Screen Objects

Customize the home screen by adding, deleting, or moving objects. Click <u>Types of Home Screen Objects</u> to learn more about objects. To add an object to a home screen:

1. Touch the ✚ icon at the top right of the home screen. The Add to Home screen menu appears, as shown in <u>Figure 7</u>.

Figure 8: Line Spacing Buttons Outlined

7. Adjusting the Font Size

If you have trouble seeing the text, try enlarging the font size. Alternatively, if you find yourself having to turn the page too often, try decreasing the font size. To adjust the font size:

1. Touch the screen anywhere. The eBook Control buttons appear in the upper right-hand corner of the screen.
2. Touch **Aa** in the upper right-hand corner of the screen. The eBook settings appear at the bottom of the screen.
3. Touch the ⊞ button to increase the font size, or touch the ⊟ button to decrease it, as outlined in **Figure 9**. The font size is adjusted accordingly.

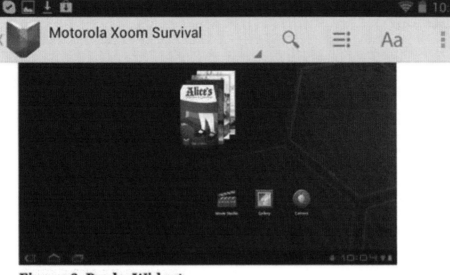

Figure 6: Books Widget

Back to Top

6. Organizing Home Screen Objects

Customize the home screen by adding, deleting, or moving objects. Click Types of Home Screen Objects to learn more about objects. To add an object to a home screen:

1. Touch the ✛ icon at the top right of the home screen. The Add to Home screen menu appears, as shown in Figure 7.

Figure 9: Font Size Buttons Outlined

8. Searching the Library (Play Books for the Nexus 7)

If you have many eBooks in your library, it may be easier to find a specific one by performing a search. To search the library in Play Books:

1. Touch the icon in the upper right-hand corner of the Play Books Home screen. The Search field is selected.
2. Enter a title or author. Matching search results appear as you type, as shown in **Figure 10**.
3. Touch a search result. The eBook opens.

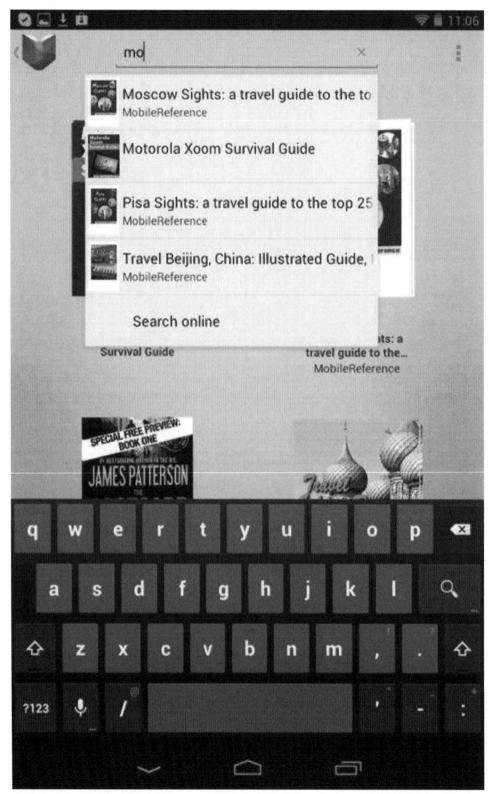

Figure 10: Matching Search Results

9. Viewing eBook Information (Play Books for the Nexus 7)

You may view an eBook's description at any time. Touch and hold the title or cover of the eBook until the eBook menu appears, as shown in **Figure 11**. Touch **About this book**. The eBook description appears.

Figure 11: eBook Menu

10. Removing eBooks from Your Device (Play Books for the Nexus 7)

You may delete any eBook from the Play Books application. Touch and hold an eBook until the eBook menu appears, and then touch **Remove from my library**. The eBook is removed. Open the Play Books market to re-download the eBook. Refer to *"Buying eBooks"* on page 207 to learn more about downloading eBooks from the Play Books market.

Note: You will not need to pay for the eBook if you wish to download it at a later date.

11. Making eBooks Available Offline (Play Books for the Nexus 7)

Some eBooks may require you to be connected to the Internet to read them. To make one of these eBooks available offline, touch and hold the eBook until the eBook menu appears. Touch **Make available offline**. The eBook can now be read without an Internet connection.

Adjusting the Settings

Wireless Settings

Table of Contents

1. Turning Airplane Mode On or Off

Putting the Nexus 7 in Airplane mode turns off Near Field Communication (NFC), which allows the device to wirelessly send data to other devices. However, Wi-Fi is still available while in Airplane mode and can be used normally. Use Airplane mode to save battery life or while flying. To turn on Airplane mode:

1. Touch the ▨ icon on the Home screen, or touch the ⊞ icon and then touch the ▨ icon. The Settings screen appears, as shown in **Figure 1**.
2. Touch **More** under 'Wireless & networks'. The Wireless Settings screen appears, as shown in **Figure 2**.
3. Touch **Airplane mode**. A ✓ mark appears and Airplane mode is turned on.
4. Touch **Airplane mode** again. The ✓ mark disappears and Airplane mode is turned off.

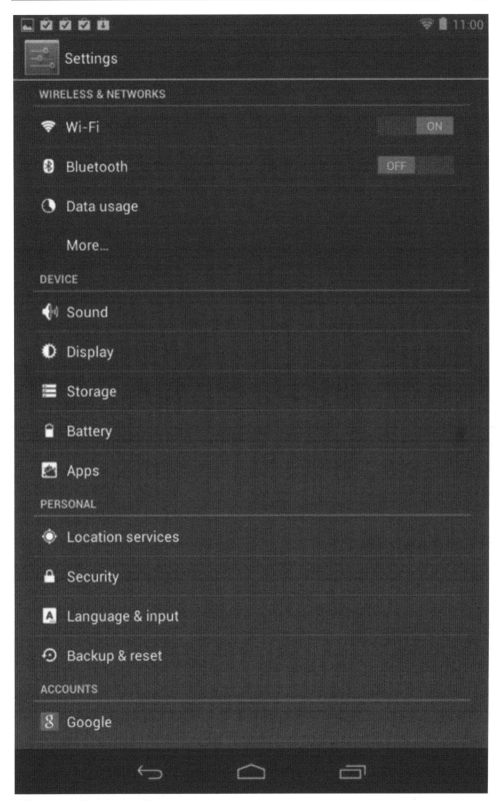

Figure 1: Settings Screen

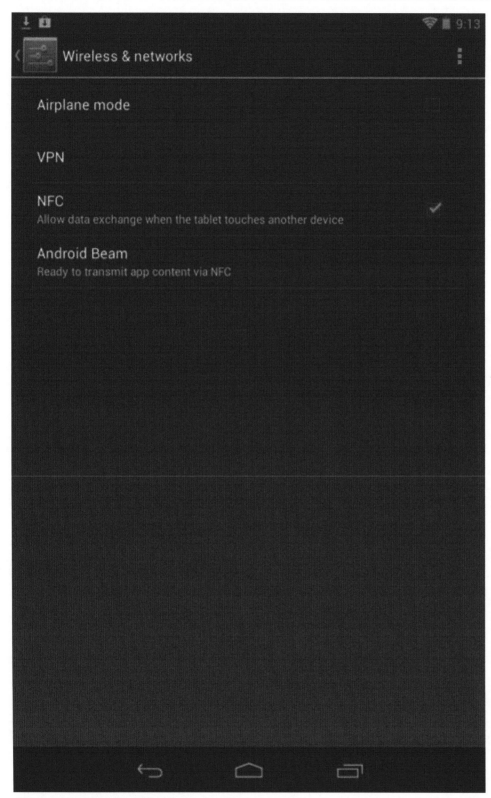

Figure 2: Wireless Settings Screen

2. Connecting to an Alternate Wi-Fi Network

The Nexus 7 can connect to Wi-Fi when it is near a hotspot. If you have performed all of the steps in *"Performing First-Time Setup"* on page 16, then you are already connected to a Wi-Fi network. To connect to an alternate Wi-Fi network:

1. Touch the ⊞ icon. The Add to Home screen appears.

2. Touch the ▦ icon. The Settings screen appears. Refer to *"Tips and Tricks"* on page 299 to learn how to quickly access the Settings screen.
3. Touch **Wi-Fi**. A list of available Wi-Fi networks appears, as shown in **Figure 3**.
4. Touch the network that has 'Connected' written below it, as outlined in **Figure 3**. The Network Status window appears, as shown in **Figure 4**.
5. Touch **Forget**. The Nexus 7 disconnects from the selected network.
6. Touch the name of a network. If the network is secured, the Wi-Fi Network Password prompt appears, as shown in **Figure 5**.
7. Enter the network password (usually found on your wireless router) and touch **Connect**. The Nexus 7 connects to the network, provided that the password you entered is correct. If the password is incorrect, 'Authenticating' will appear next to the name of the network indefinitely.

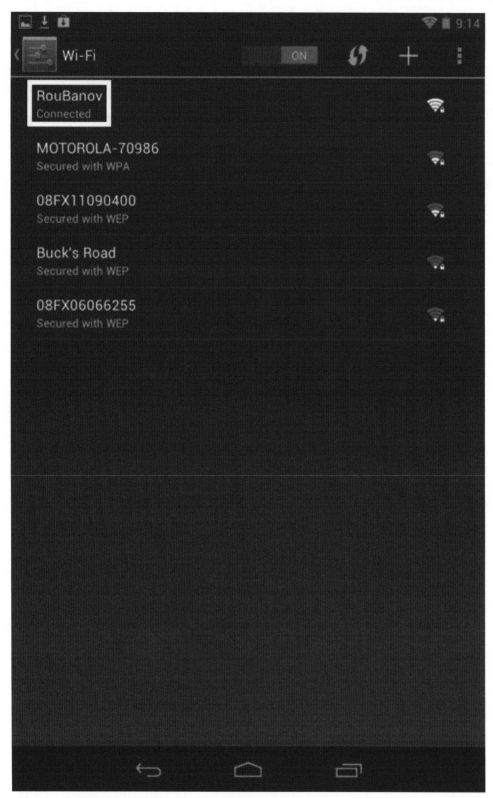

Figure 3: List of Available Wi-Fi Networks

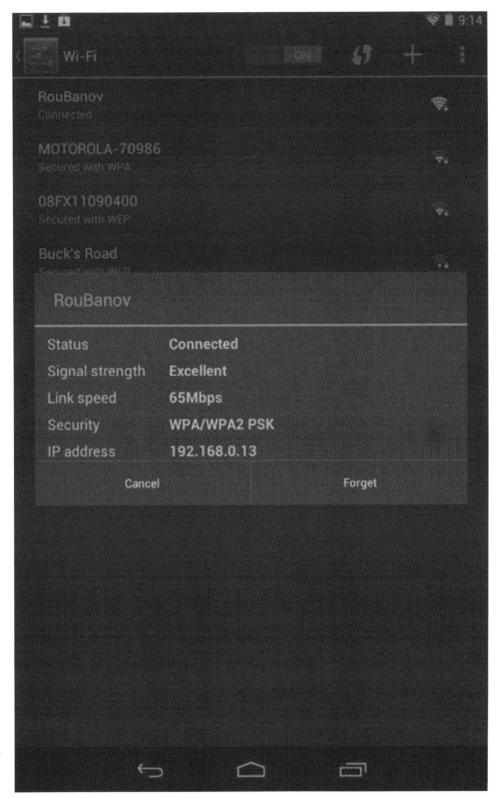

Figure 4: Network Status Window

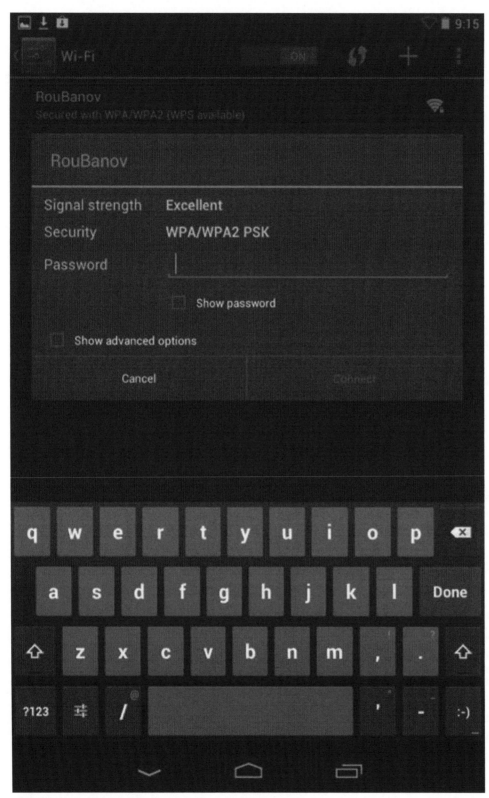

Figure 5: Wi-Fi Network Password Prompt

3. Using Bluetooth

Bluetooth allows the Nexus 7 to communicate with other mobile devices. To turn on Bluetooth and pair with another device:

1. Touch the ![icon] icon on the Home screen, or touch the ![icon] icon and then touch the ![icon] icon. The Settings screen appears.
2. Touch **Bluetooth**. The Bluetooth Settings screen appears, as shown in **Figure 6**.
3. Touch the OFF switch at the top of the screen, as outlined in **Figure 6**. The ON switch appears and Bluetooth is turned on. A list of available devices appears that are in close proximity to the Nexus 7 and also have their Bluetooth turned on. Make sure the secondary device is ready to pair.
4. Touch a device in the list. The Bluetooth Pairing Request window appears, as shown in **Figure 7**.
5. Make sure both devices are displaying the same pass key and touch **Pair** on each one. The Nexus 7 is paired with the secondary device.
6. Touch the ON switch at the top of the screen. Bluetooth is turned off.

Figure 6: Bluetooth Settings Screen

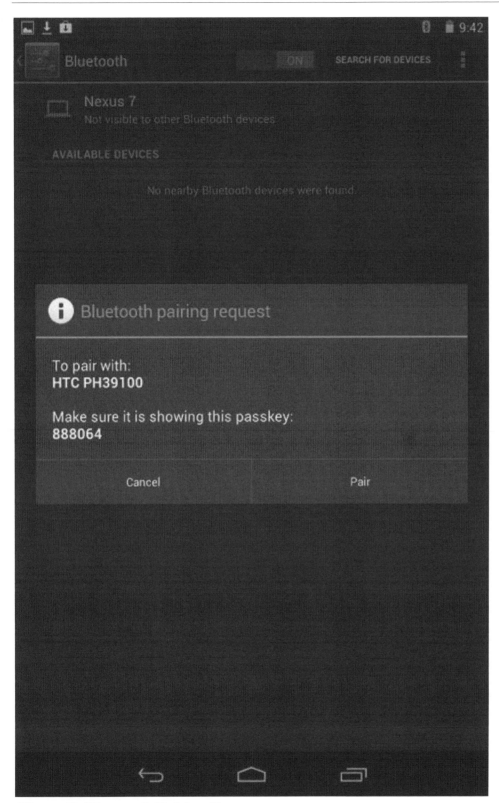

Figure 7: Bluetooth Pairing Request

4. Wirelessly Transferring Data to Another Device

The Nexus 7 can transfer data to another mobile device without the use of Bluetooth or email. By using the Android Beam feature, you can transfer data by holding your Nexus 7 back to back with another Android Beam-enabled device. To wirelessly transfer data using the Android Beam feature:

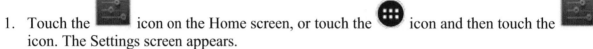

1. Touch the icon on the Home screen, or touch the icon and then touch the icon. The Settings screen appears.
2. Touch **More** under 'Wireless & Networks'. The Wireless Settings screen appears.
3. Touch **NFC**. A mark appears and NFC is turned on.
4. Touch **Android Beam**. The Android Beam screen appears, as shown in **Figure 8**.
5. Touch the OFF switch at the top of the screen, as outlined in **Figure 8**. The ON switch appears and the Android Beam feature is turned on. You are now ready to wirelessly transfer data.

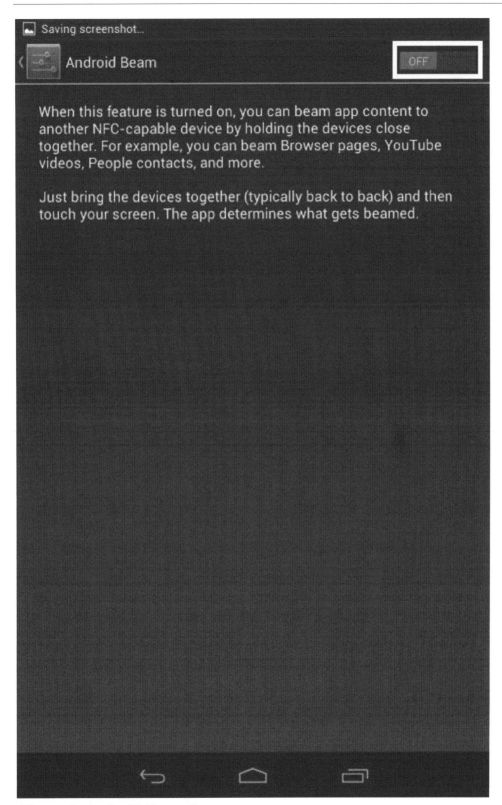

Figure 8: Android Beam Screen

Sound Settings

Table of Contents

1. Adjusting the Notification, Media, and Alarm Volume

The volumes for various notifications can be set separately. To set the various Notification volumes:

1. Touch the ![icon] icon on the Home screen, or touch the ![icon] icon and then touch the ![icon] icon. The Settings screen appears, as shown in **Figure 1**.
2. Touch **Sound**. The Sound Settings screen appears, as shown in **Figure 2**.
3. Touch **Volumes**. The Volume Controls appear, as shown in **Figure 3**.

4. Touch one of the sliders and drag it to the left or right, to decrease or increase the corresponding Notification volume, respectively. The volume is adjusted.

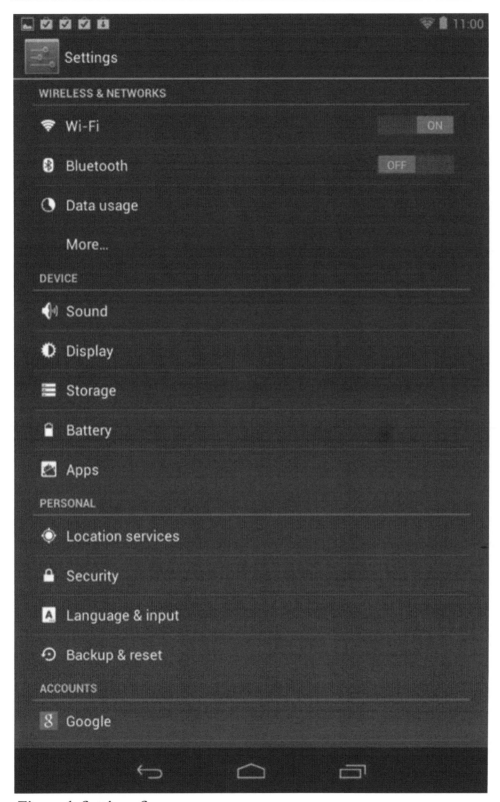

Figure 1: Settings Screen

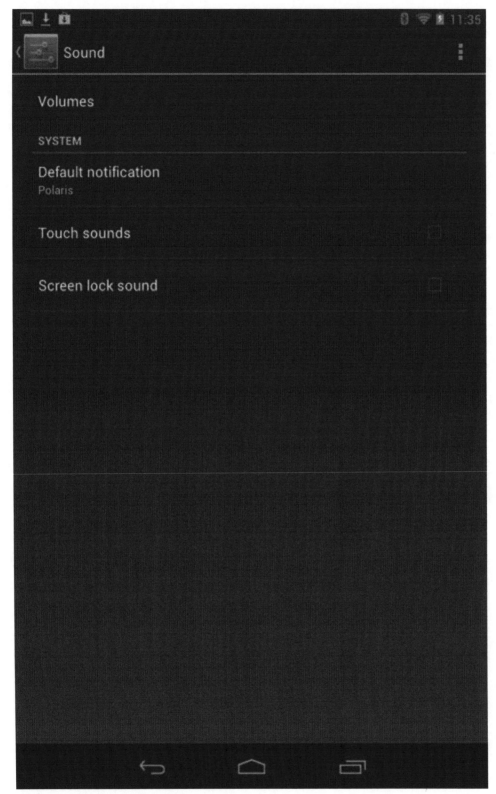

Figure 2: Sound Settings Screen

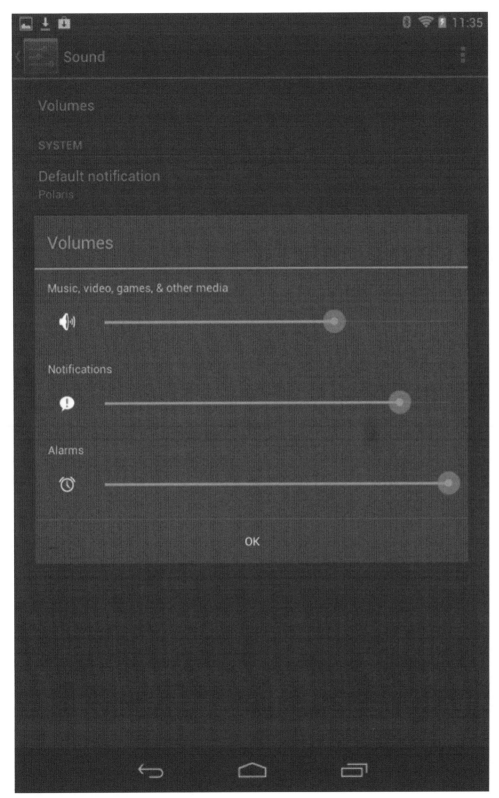

Figure 3: Volume Controls

2. Changing the Notification Ringtone

The default ringtone that is used for all notifications can be changed. To set the Notification ringtone:

1. Touch the 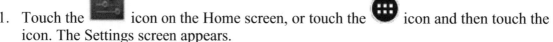 icon on the Home screen, or touch the icon and then touch the icon. The Settings screen appears.
2. Touch **Sound**. The Sound Settings screen appears.
3. Touch **Default notification**. A list of Notification ringtones appears, as shown in **Figure 4**.
4. Touch a ringtone. A preview of the ringtone plays.
5. Touch **OK**. The new Notification ringtone is set. Alternatively, touch **Cancel** to return to using the previously set ringtone.

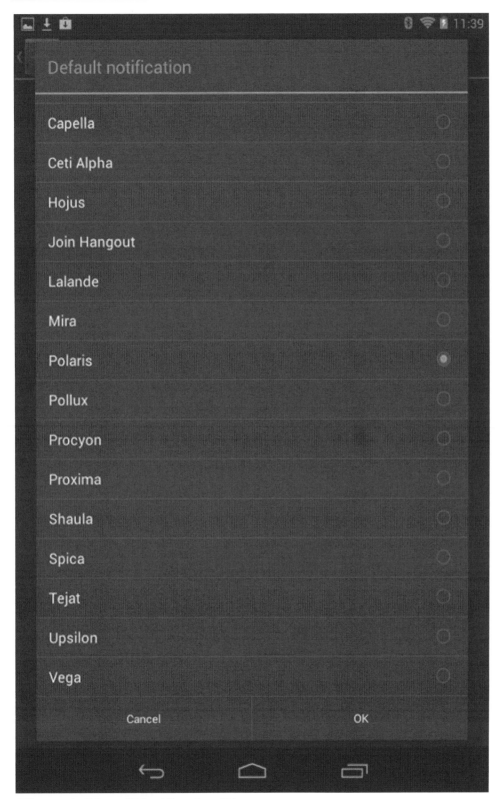

Figure 4: List of Notification Ringtones

3. Turning Touch Sounds On or Off

When any selection is made on the touchscreen, the Nexus 7 can play a confirmation sound. To turn on Touch Sounds:

1. Touch the [icon] icon on the Home screen, or touch the [icon] icon and then touch the [icon] icon. The Settings screen appears.
2. Touch **Sound**. The Sound Settings screen appears.
3. Touch **Touch sounds**. A [✓] mark appears and Touch Sounds are turned on.
4. Touch **Touch sounds** again. The [✓] mark disappears and Touch Sounds are turned off.

4. Turning Screen Lock Sounds On or Off

When the screen is locked or unlocked, the Nexus 7 can play a sound. To turn on Screen Lock sounds:

1. Touch the [icon] icon on the Home screen, or touch the [icon] icon and then touch the [icon] icon. The Settings screen appears.
2. Touch **Sound**. The Sound Settings screen appears.
3. Touch **Screen lock sound**. A [✓] mark appears and Screen Lock Sounds are turned on.
4. Touch **Screen lock sound** again. The [✓] mark disappears and Screen Lock Sounds are turned off.

Screen Settings

Table of Contents

1. Adjusting the Brightness

The Nexus 7 can be set to automatically detect light conditions by using the built-in light sensor and then set the brightness accordingly. When Automatic Brightness is turned off, you may manually adjust the brightness. To customize the brightness:

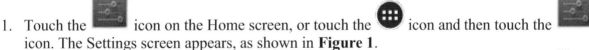

1. Touch the ▦ icon on the Home screen, or touch the ⊞ icon and then touch the ▦ icon. The Settings screen appears, as shown in **Figure 1**.
2. Touch **Display**. The Display Settings screen appears, as shown in **Figure 2**.
3. Touch **Brightness**. The Brightness window appears, as shown in **Figure 3**. By default, Automatic Brightness is turned on.
4. Touch **Automatic brightness**. The ✓ mark disappears and you may now manually adjust the brightness.
5. Touch and drag the ● slider to the left or right. The brightness is decreased or increased, respectively.
6. Touch **OK**. The brightness is adjusted.
7. Touch **Automatic brightness** again if you would rather have the device determine the optimal brightness. A ✓ mark appears and Automatic Brightness is turned on.

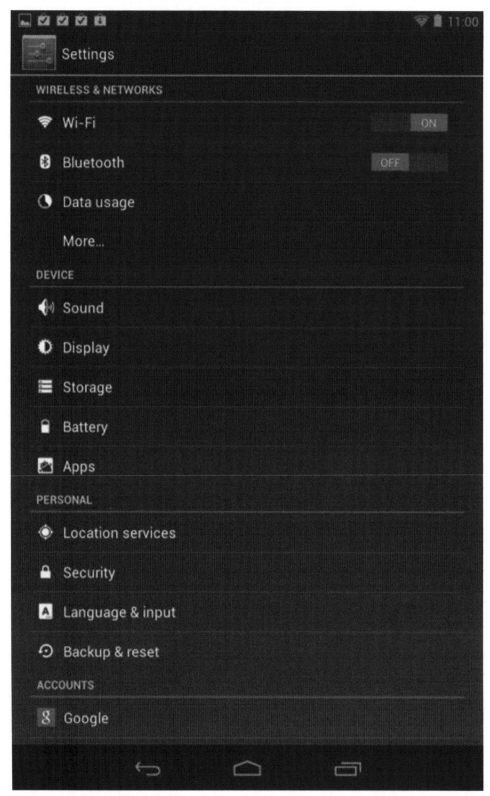

Figure 1: Settings Screen

Figure 2: Display Settings Screen

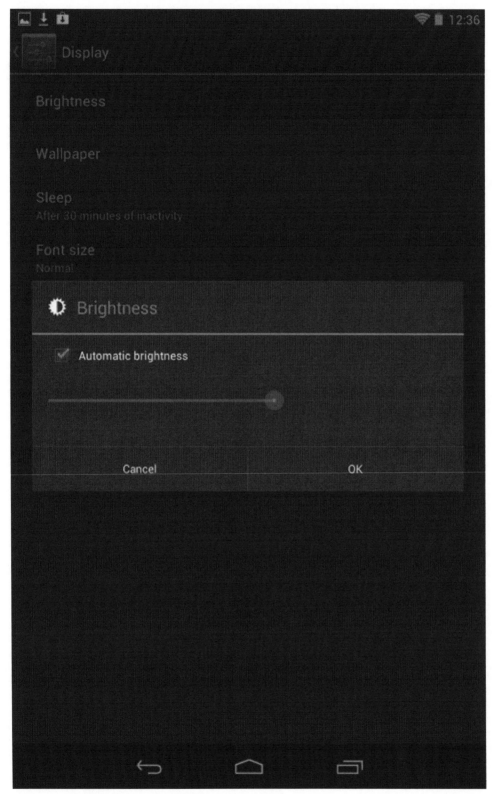

Figure 3: Brightness Window

2. Turning Automatic Screen Rotation On or Off

By default, the Nexus 7 will rotate the screen every time the device is rotated from the horizontal to the vertical position and vice versa (except when viewing a Home screen). To turn Automatic Screen Rotation on or off:

1. Drag down the Status bar (the bar containing the clock and battery meter), which is located at the top of the screen. The Status bar displays the time and battery level. The Notifications Center appears, as shown in **Figure 4**.

2. Touch the ⟳ icon at the top of the screen, as outlined in **Figure 4**. The 🔒 icon appears and Automatic Screen Rotation is turned off.

3. Touch the 🔒 icon. The ⟳ icon appears and Automatic Screen Rotation is turned on.

Note: Refer to "Viewing the Home Screens in Landscape View" *on page 307 to learn how to rotate the Home screens.*

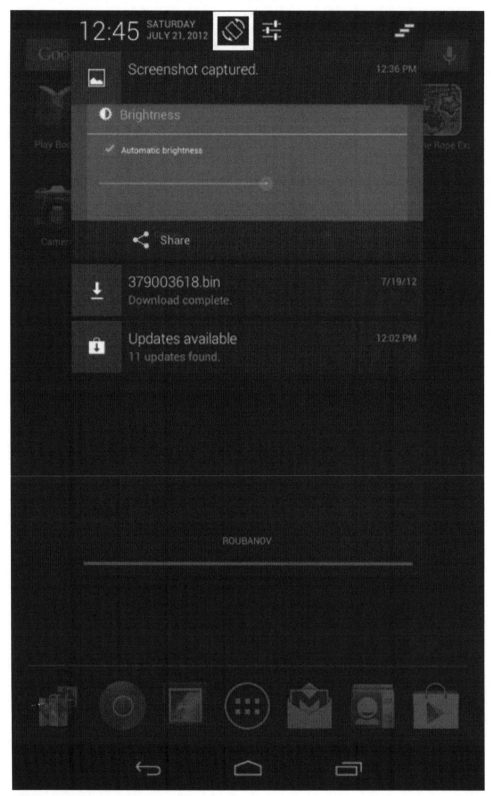

Figure 4: Notifications Center

3. Changing the Wallpaper

The wallpaper is the image that is displayed in the background on the Lock and Home screens. To change the wallpaper:

1. Touch and hold an empty spot on any Home screen. The Wallpaper Source window appears, as shown in **Figure 5**.
2. Touch **Gallery**, **Live Wallpapers**, or **Wallpapers**. The corresponding source appears.
3. Touch the desired image and then touch **Set wallpaper** at the bottom of the screen if you are choosing from the 'Wallpapers' or 'Live Wallpapers' source. If choosing from the Gallery, crop the image using the techniques described in *"Cropping a Picture"* on page 65 and then touch **OK** in the upper right-hand corner of the screen. The wallpaper is changed.

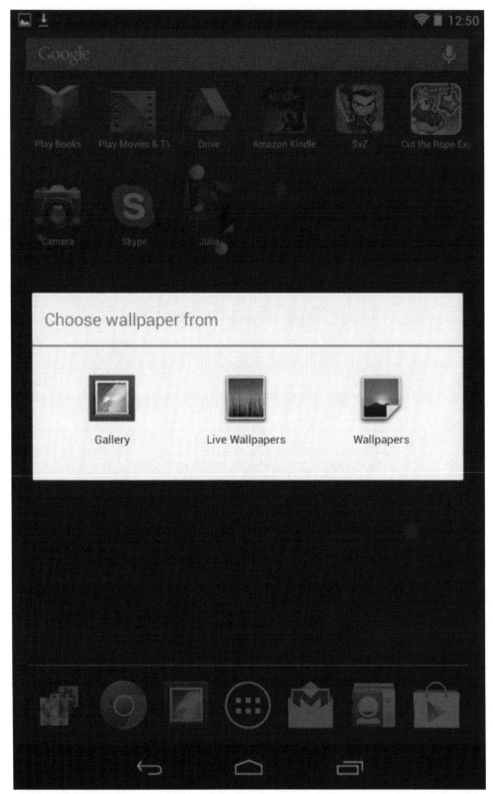

Figure 5: Wallpaper Source Window

4. Setting the Amount of Time Before the Device Nexus 7 Locks Itself

The Sleep Timer determines the amount of time that passes before the screen goes black and the Nexus 7 is automatically locked. To set the Sleep Timer:

1. Touch the [icon] icon on the Home screen, or touch the [icon] icon and then touch the [icon] icon. The Settings screen appears.
2. Touch **Display**. The Display Settings screen appears.
3. Touch **Sleep**. The Sleep Timer options appear, as shown in **Figure 6**.
4. Touch an option in the list. The Sleep Timer is set.

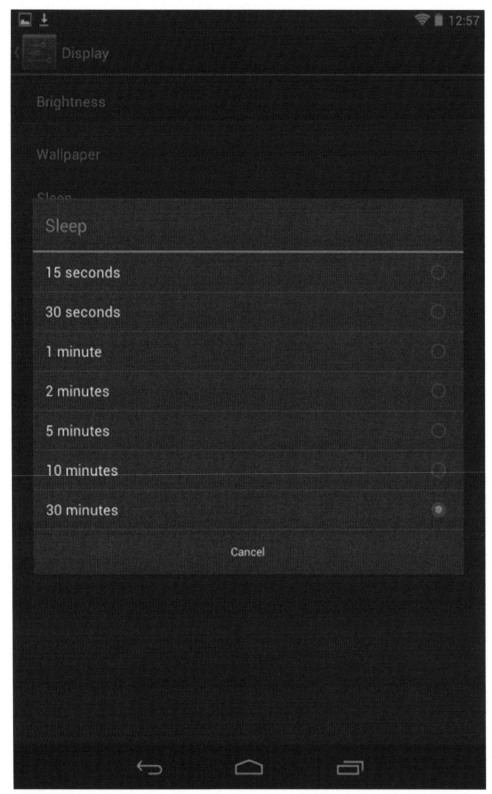

Figure 6: Sleep Timer Options

5. Adjusting the Font Size

If you have trouble seeing text in menus and applications, try increasing the font size. To adjust the font size:

1. Touch the icon on the Home screen, or touch the icon and then touch the icon. The Settings screen appears.
2. Touch **Display**. The Display Settings screen appears.
3. Touch **Font size**. A list of available font sizes appears, as shown in **Figure 7**.
4. Touch one of the options in the list. The font size is adjusted.

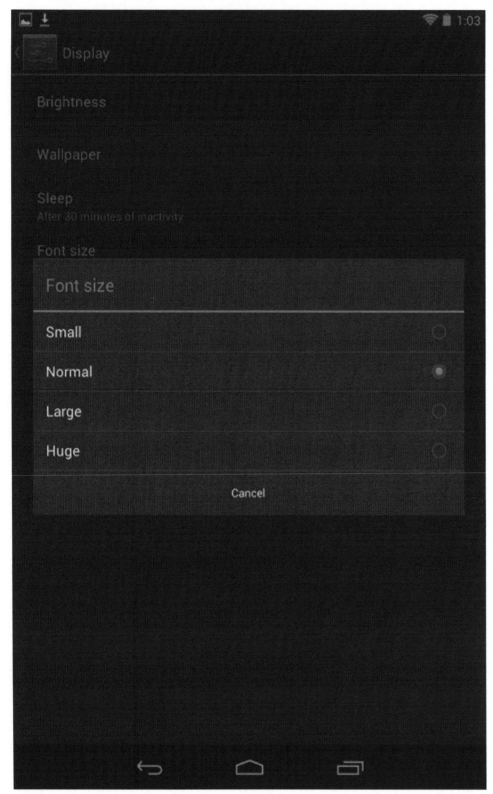

Figure 7: List of Available Font Sizes

Security Settings

Table of Contents

1. Locking the Screen with a Slider

Prevent the Nexus 7 from waking up accidentally by setting up a Slider Lock. Note that a Slider Lock does not prevent unauthorized users from accessing your Nexus 7. Refer to one of the next four sections to learn how to prevent unauthorized users from accessing your device. To set up a Slider Lock:

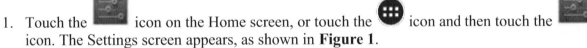

1. Touch the ⬛ icon on the Home screen, or touch the ⬛ icon and then touch the ⬛ icon. The Settings screen appears, as shown in **Figure 1**.
2. Touch **Security**. The Security Settings screen appears, as shown in **Figure 2**.
3. Touch **Screen lock**. The Screen Lock Settings screen appears, as shown in **Figure 3**. If a screen lock has already been set up, you will need to enter the corresponding passcode or pattern before proceeding.
4. Touch **Slide**. The device will be locked using a basic slider. To unlock it, touch and hold

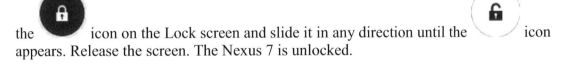

the ⬤ icon on the Lock screen and slide it in any direction until the 🔓 icon appears. Release the screen. The Nexus 7 is unlocked.

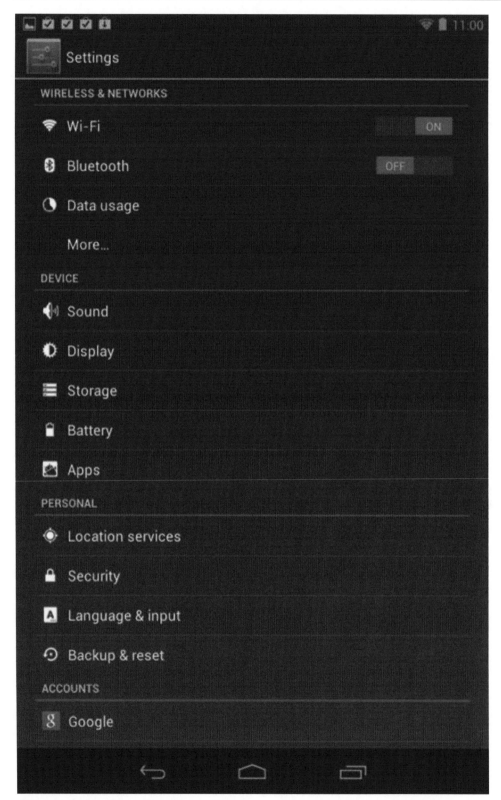

Figure 1: Settings Screen

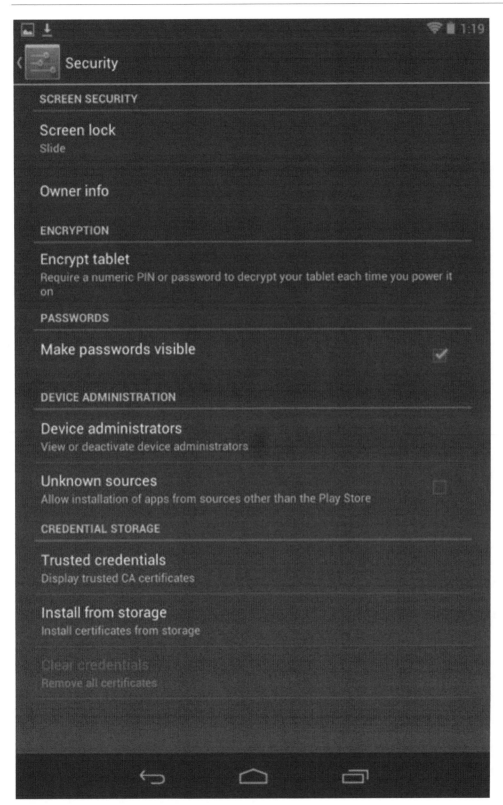

Figure 2: Security Settings Screen

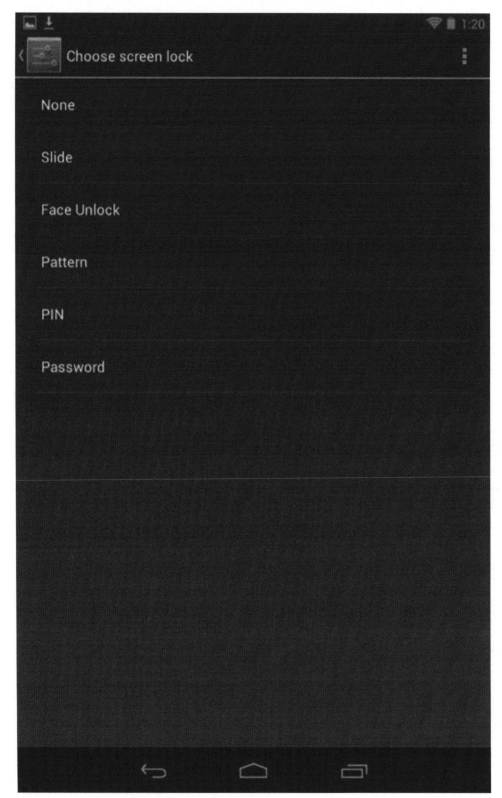

Figure 3: Screen Lock Settings Screen

2. Locking the Screen with an Alphanumeric Password

In order to prevent unauthorized users from accessing your Nexus 7, you may wish to lock the device using an alphanumeric (letters and numbers) password. To lock the screen using an alphanumeric password:

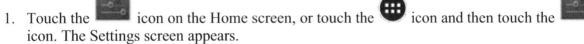

1. Touch the icon on the Home screen, or touch the icon and then touch the icon. The Settings screen appears.
2. Touch **Security**. The Security Settings screen appears.
3. Touch **Screen lock**. The Screen Lock Settings screen appears. If a screen lock has already been set up, you will need to enter the corresponding passcode or pattern before proceeding.
4. Touch **Password**. The Password Selection screen appears, as shown in **Figure 4**.
5. Enter the desired password, which must be a combination of letters and numbers that is at least 4 and no more than 16 characters in length. Touch **Continue**. The Password Confirmation screen appears.
6. Enter the same password again. Touch **OK**. The Password lock is set. The password will be required to unlock the screen.

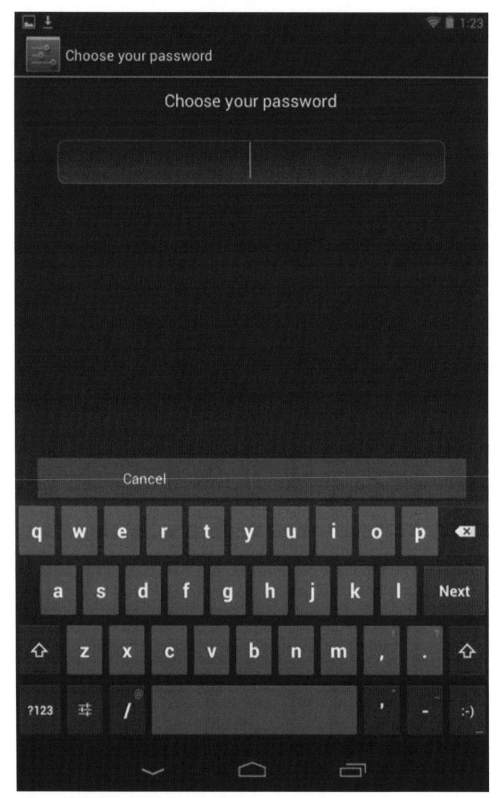

Figure 4: Password Selection Screen

3. Locking the Screen with a Personal Identification Number (PIN)

In order to prevent unauthorized users from accessing your Nexus 7, you may wish to lock the device using a numeric PIN. To lock the screen using a PIN:

1. Touch the ▦ icon on the Home screen, or touch the ⊕ icon and then touch the ▦ icon. The Settings screen appears.
2. Touch **Security**. The Security Settings screen appears.
3. Touch **Screen lock**. The Screen Lock Settings screen appears. If a screen lock has already been set up, you will need to enter the corresponding passcode or pattern before proceeding.
4. Touch **PIN**. The PIN Selection screen appears, as shown in **Figure 5**.
5. Enter the desired PIN, which must be at least 4 and no more than 16 digits in length. Touch Continue. The PIN Confirmation screen appears.
6. Enter the same PIN again. Touch **OK**. The PIN lock is set. The PIN will be required to unlock the screen.

Figure 5: PIN Selection Screen

4. Locking the Screen with a Pattern

In order to prevent unauthorized users from accessing your Nexus 7, you may wish to lock the device using a pattern. To lock the screen using a pattern:

1. Touch the ![icon] icon on the Home screen, or touch the ![icon] icon and then touch the ![icon] icon. The Settings screen appears.
2. Touch **Security**. The Security Settings screen appears.
3. Touch **Screen lock**. The Screen Lock Settings screen appears. If a screen lock has already been set up, you will need to enter the corresponding passcode or pattern before proceeding.
4. Touch **Pattern**. The Pattern Selection screen appears, as shown in **Figure 6**.
5. Draw the desired pattern. Touch **Continue**. The Pattern Confirmation screen appears.
6. Draw the same pattern again. Touch **Confirm**. The Pattern lock is set. The pattern will be required to unlock the screen.

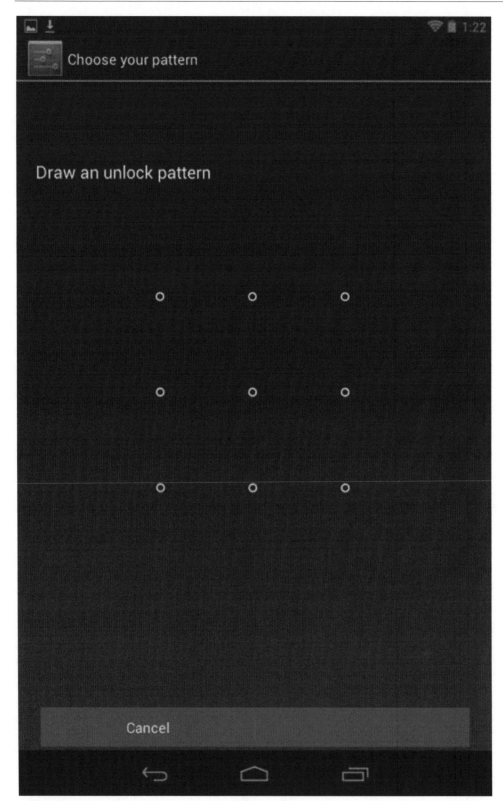

Figure 6: Pattern Selection Screen

5. Locking the Screen with Your Face

In order to prevent unauthorized users from accessing your Nexus 7, you may wish to lock the device using your face in the front-facing camera. To lock the screen using your face:

1. Touch the ![icon] icon on the Home screen, or touch the ⊞ icon and then touch the icon. The Settings screen appears.
2. Touch **Security**. The Security Settings screen appears.
3. Touch **Screen lock**. The Screen Lock Settings screen appears. If a screen lock has already been set up, you will need to enter the corresponding passcode or pattern before proceeding.
4. Touch **Face Unlock**. The Face Unlock screen appears.
5. Touch **Set it up** at the bottom of the screen. Several suggestions for capturing your face appear.
6. Touch **Continue** at the bottom of the screen. The camera turns on and a white dotted oval appears.
7. Align your face so that it is within the white dotted oval, as shown in **Figure 7**. The device analyzes your face. When finished, the Face Confirmation screen appears, as shown in **Figure 8**.
8. Touch **Continue** at the bottom of the screen. The Backup Lock screen appears. You will need to enter an alternate lock, which will be used in case you cannot unlock the screen with your face. For instance, unlocking the screen using your face may be difficult when you are in a dark place or after having plastic surgery.
9. Touch **Pattern** or **PIN** to set up the corresponding lock. Refer to *"Locking the Screen with a Pattern"* on page 267 or *"Locking the Screen with a Personal Identification Number (PIN)"* on page 265 to learn how to set up a Pattern or a PIN lock. The Face lock is set. Show your face in the camera any time you wish to unlock the screen.

Figure 7: Aligning Your Face

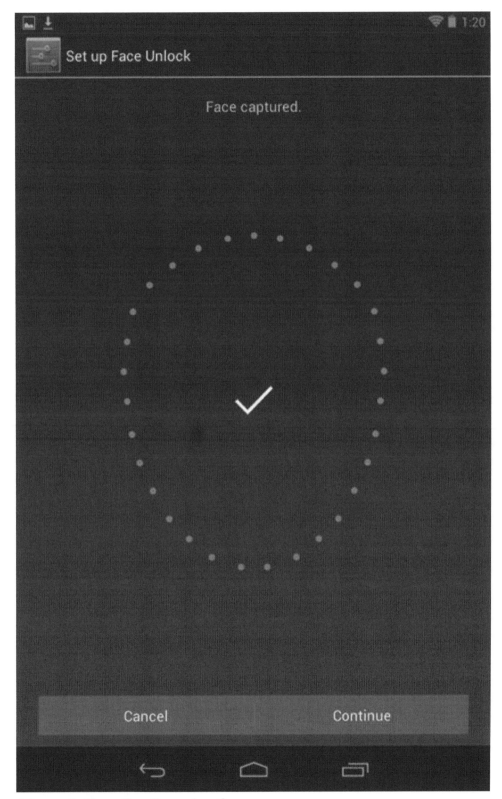

Figure 8: Face Confirmation Screen

6. Checking to Make Sure the Face Unlocking the Screen is Alive (Face Lock Only)

In order to prevent unauthorized users from unlocking your Nexus 7 by using a picture of your face, you may turn on the Liveness Check feature. Liveness Check will make sure that the person looking at the camera is alive by requiring a blink before unlocking the screen. Sometimes, you will need to blink more than once to unlock the screen. To turn Liveness Check on or off:

1. Set up a Face lock. Refer to *"Locking the Screen with Your Face"* on page 269 to learn how.

2. Touch **Liveness check** on the Security Settings screen. A ✓ mark appears and Liveness Check is turned on.

3. Touch **Liveness check** again. The Pattern or PIN screen appears.

4. Draw the pattern or enter the PIN that you set up when setting up the Face lock. The ✓ mark disappears and Liveness Check is turned off.

7. Encrypting the Nexus 7

The Nexus 7 can encrypt all of the data stored in its memory and require a password to decrypt the data each time it is powered on. To encrypt the data on the Nexus 7:

1. Touch the [icon] icon on the Home screen, or touch the [icon] icon and then touch the [icon] icon. The Settings screen appears.

2. Touch **Security**. The Security Settings screen appears.

3. Touch **Encrypt tablet**. The Data Encryption screen appears, as shown in **Figure 9**.

4. Using the included charging adapter, plug the Nexus 7 into a power outlet, or use a MicroUSB to USB cable to plug it into a USB port on a computer. Touch **Encrypt tablet** and leave it plugged in to a power source to make sure that the battery does not die while data is being encrypted. The tablet may take more than an hour to encrypt.

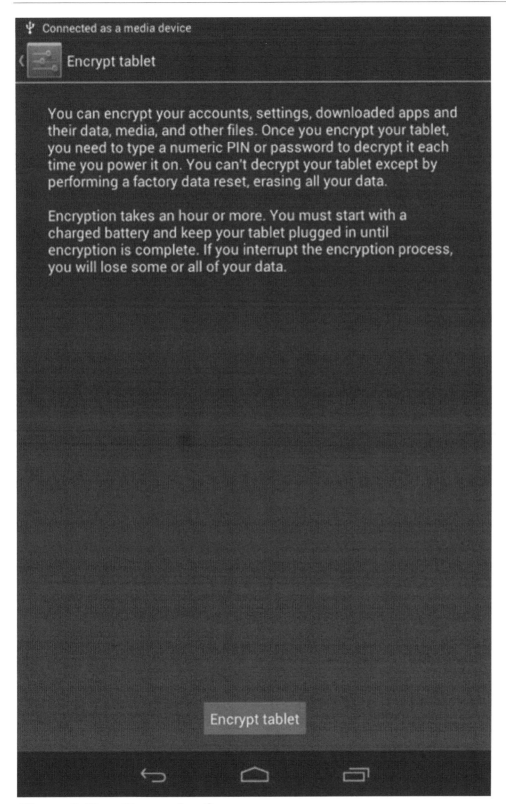

Figure 9: Data Encryption Screen

8. Turning Password Visibility On or Off

When entering passwords on the Nexus 7, they can be concealed in case there is somebody else looking at the screen. Otherwise, it may be more convenient to see what is being typed. Passwords are visible by default. To turn Password Visibility on or off:

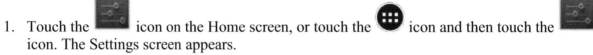

1. Touch the ![icon] icon on the Home screen, or touch the ⊞ icon and then touch the ![icon] icon. The Settings screen appears.
2. Touch **Security**. The Security Settings screen appears.
3. Scroll down and touch **Make passwords visible**. A ✔ mark appears and passwords will be visible.
4. Touch **Make passwords visible** again. The ✔ mark disappears and passwords will be concealed.

Language and Input Settings

Table of Contents

1. Selecting a Language

The Nexus 7 can display menus and applications that come pre-installed on the device, such as Gmail, in any one of 41 languages. To select a language:

1. Touch the ▦ icon on the Home screen, or touch the ⊞ icon and then touch the ▦ icon. The Settings screen appears, as shown in **Figure 1**.
2. Touch **Language & input**. The Language & Input Settings screen appears, as shown in **Figure 2**.
3. Touch **Language**. A list of available languages appears, as shown in **Figure 3**.
4. Touch a language in the list. The language is set and will be used in all menus on the device.

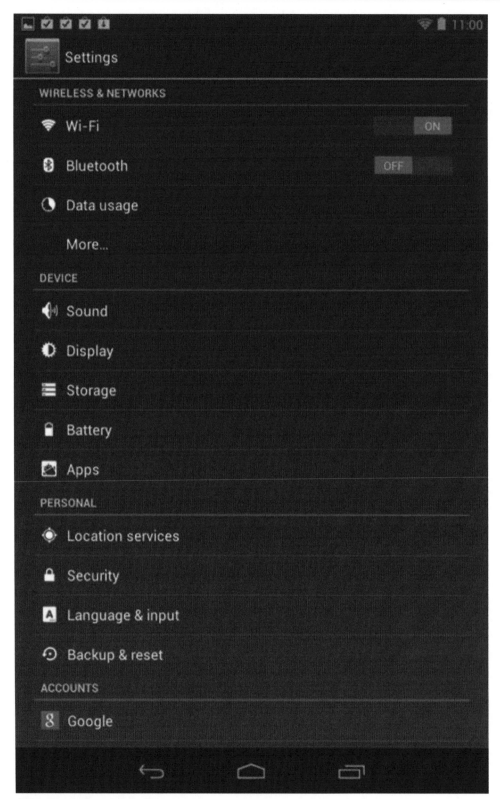

Figure 1: Settings Screen

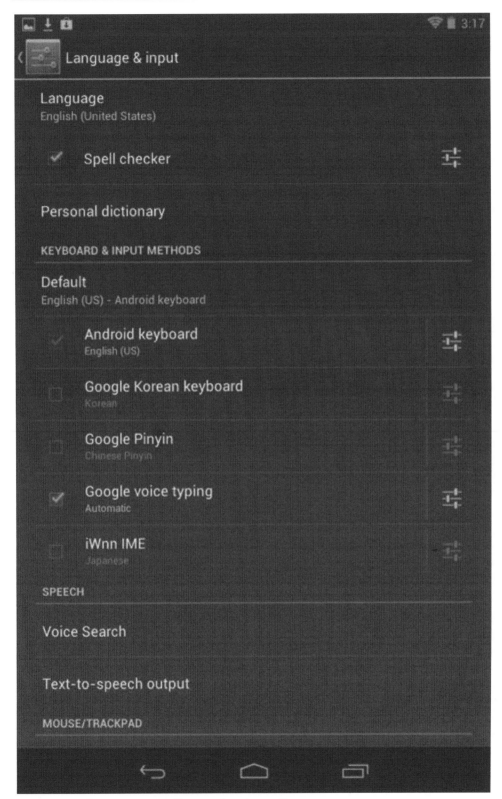

Figure 2: Language & Input Settings Screen

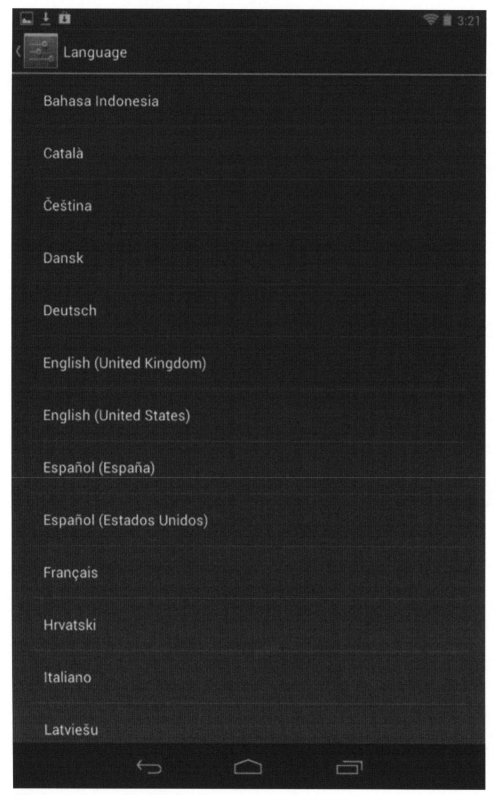

Figure 3: List of Available Languages

2. Turning Spell Checking On or Off

The Nexus 7 can check the spelling of words that you type. To turn Spell Checking on or off:

1. Touch the 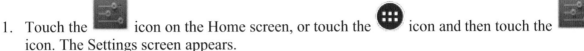 icon on the Home screen, or touch the icon and then touch the icon. The Settings screen appears.
2. Touch **Language & input**. The Language & Input Settings screen appears.
3. Touch **Spell checker**. A ✔ mark appears and the Spell Checker is turned on.
4. Touch **Spell checker** again. The ✔ mark disappears and the Spell Checker is turned off.

3. Adding Words and Phrases to the Personal Dictionary

The Nexus 7 can store words in a Personal Dictionary to suggest them while you're typing. You can also add shortcuts to phrases to the personal dictionary, such as "brb" for "be right back." To add an entry to the user dictionary:

1. Touch the icon on the Home screen, or touch the icon and then touch the icon. The Settings screen appears.
2. Touch **Language & input**. The Language & Input Settings screen appears.
3. Touch **Personal dictionary**. The Personal Dictionary appears, as shown in **Figure 4** (with three words already added).
4. Touch the ✛ icon in the upper right-hand corner of the screen. The Add to Dictionary screen appears, as shown in **Figure 5**.
5. Enter a word or phrase and touch the Next button. The 'Shortcut' field is selected.
6. Enter an optional shortcut, which can be a series of letters or numbers that will be substituted with the entire word or phrase that you entered in the previous step. The shortcut is entered.
7. Touch the Done button. The keyboard is hidden.
8. Touch the icon in the upper left-hand corner of the screen. The word or phrase is added to the Personal Dictionary.

Figure 4: Personal Dictionary

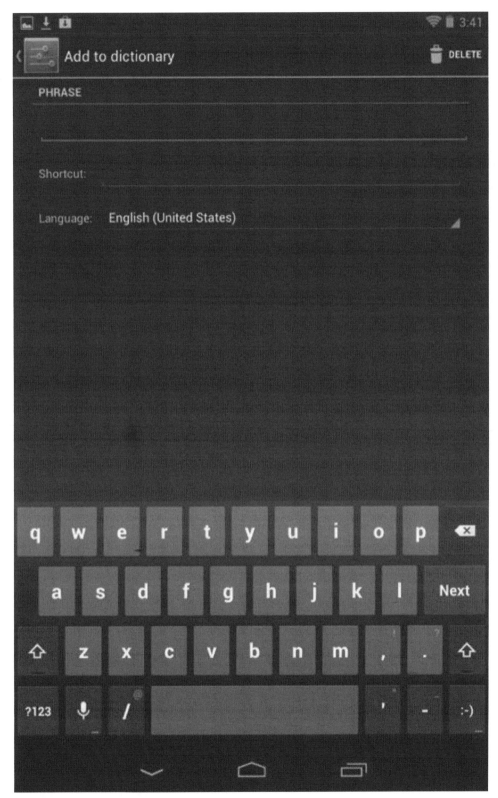

Figure 5: Add to Dictionary Screen

4. Changing the Input Method

The method that you use to input text can be changed. By default, the Android keyboard and Google voice typing are both selected; Android keyboard cannot be turned off. To change the text input method:

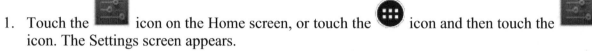

1. Touch the ![icon] icon on the Home screen, or touch the ![icon] icon and then touch the ![icon] icon. The Settings screen appears.
2. Touch **Language & input**. The Language & Input Settings screen appears.
3. Touch one of the options under 'Keyboard & Input Methods'. A ![checkmark] mark appears and the corresponding Input method is added.
4. Touch the same Input method again. The ![checkmark] mark disappears and the corresponding input method is removed.

5. Customizing Voice Search Settings

The Voice Recognition feature on the Nexus 7 can be customized to improve accuracy and filter voice results. To customize Voice Recognition settings:

1. Touch the [icon] icon on the Home screen, or touch the [icon] icon and then touch the [icon] icon. The Settings screen appears.
2. Touch **Language & input**. The Language & Input Settings screen appears.
3. Touch **Voice Search**. The Voice Search Settings screen appears, as shown in **Figure 6**.
4. Touch one of the following options to edit the setting:

-   **Language** - Sets the language to be used with the voice recognition software.

-   **Speech output** - Customizes whether Speech Output is always enabled, or is only turned on when using a hands-free device with the Nexus 7.

-   **Block offensive words** - Hides offensive words when showing voice results, even if they are recognized. A [check] mark appears to signify that the option is turned on.

-   **Hotword detection** - Launches the Voice search when using Google Now; touch and hold the [icon] key and slide your finger up to **Google** to activate Google Now. A [check] mark appears to signify that Hotword Detection is turned on.

-   **Download offline speech recognition** - Downloads additional speech recognition languages to be used offline; touch **All** at the top of the screen to view all options.

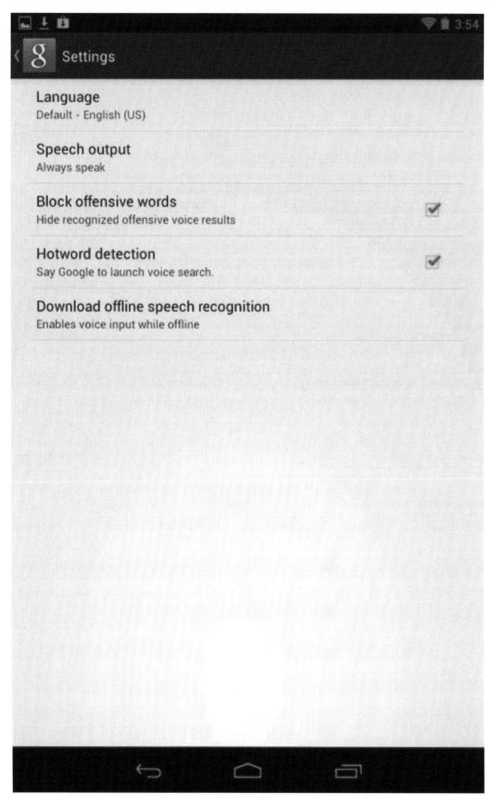

Figure 6: Voice Search Settings Screen

6. Changing the Text-to-Speech Speaking Rate

Some applications on the Nexus 7 can use the Text-to-Speech feature, which reads the text on the screen aloud. To change the speech rate of the Text-to-Speech feature:

1. Touch the icon on the Home screen, or touch the icon and then touch the icon. The Settings screen appears.
2. Touch **Language & input**. The Language & Input Settings screen appears.
3. Touch **Text-to-speech output**. The Text-to-Speech Settings screen appears, as shown in **Figure 7**.
4. Touch **Speech rate**. A list of speech rates appears, as shown in **Figure 8**.
5. Touch one of the five speeds, ranging from 'Very slow' to 'Very fast'. The rate at which the speaker pronounces the words is adjusted.

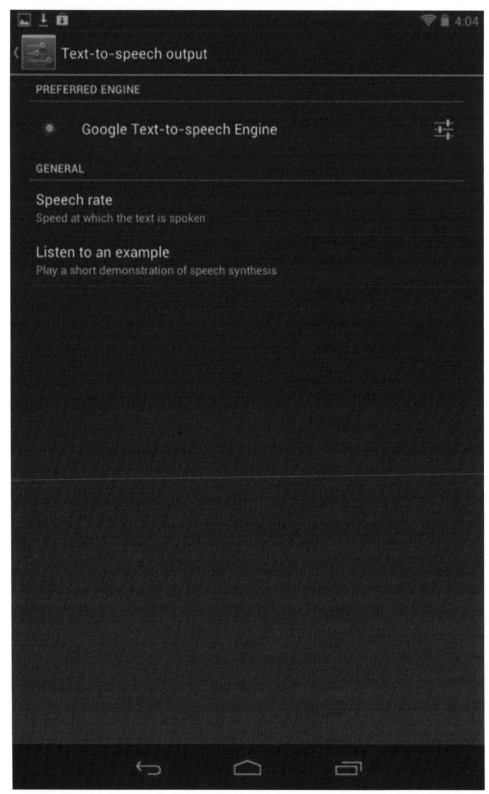

Figure 7: Text-to-Speech Settings Screen

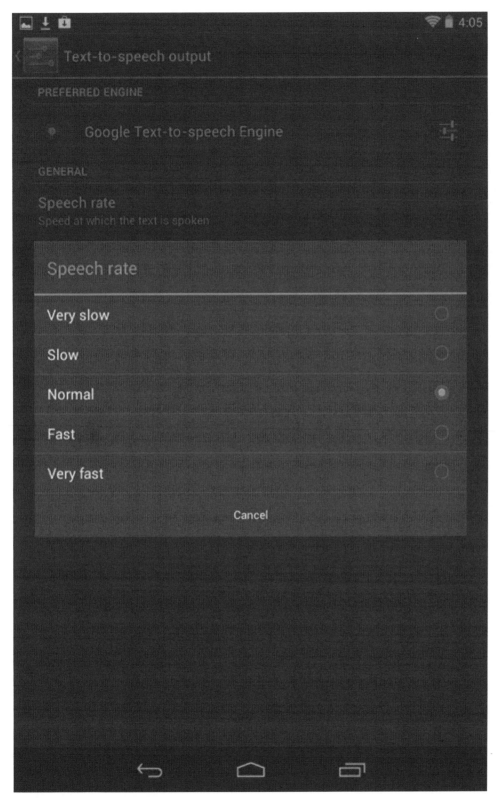

Figure 8: List of Speech Rates

7. Downloading Additional Text-to-Speech Languages

The Text-to-Speech feature can pronounce phrases in any of five languages, including English. However, languages other than English do not come pre-installed on the Nexus 7. To download additional Text-to-Speech languages:

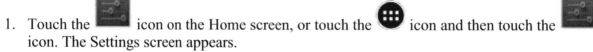

1. Touch the ▣ icon on the Home screen, or touch the ⊕ icon and then touch the ▣ icon. The Settings screen appears.
2. Touch **Language & input**. The Language & Input Settings screen appears.
3. Touch **Text-to-speech output**. The Text-to-Speech Settings screen appears.

4. Touch the ▤ icon next to 'Google Text-to-speech Engine'. The Text-to-Speech Settings screen appears, as shown in **Figure 9**.
5. Touch **Install voice data**. A list of available voice data appears, as shown in **Figure 10**.

6. Touch the **Download** button next to the language that you wish to download. The corresponding Text-to-Speech language is downloaded. The **Delete** button appears next to the language once it has been installed.

7. Touch the **Delete** button. The Text-to-Speech language is uninstalled.

Figure 9: Text-to-Speech Settings Screen

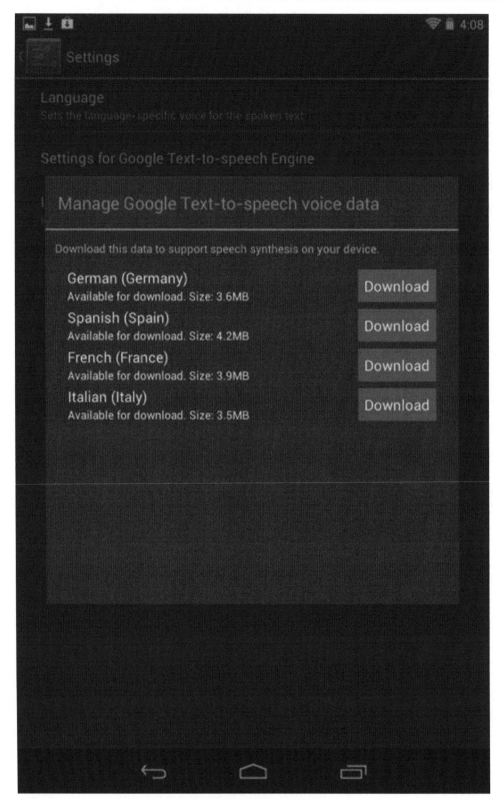

Figure 10: List of Available Voice Data

Date and Time Settings

Table of Contents

1. Manually Setting the Date, Time Zone, and Time

By default, the Nexus 7 automatically sets the time and date using the selected Time Zone setting. If you prefer an alternate Time Zone or Time setting, it may be useful to set the time, date, and time zone manually.

To turn off Automatic Date and Time and use manual settings:

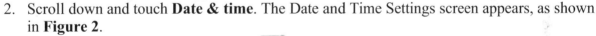

1. Touch the ⬛ icon on the Home screen, or touch the ⬤ icon and then touch the ⬛ icon. The Settings screen appears, as shown in **Figure 1**.
2. Scroll down and touch **Date & time**. The Date and Time Settings screen appears, as shown in **Figure 2**.
3. Touch **Automatic date & time**. The ✔ mark next to 'Automatic date and time' disappears and the feature is turned off. The 'Set date' and 'Set time' options are no longer grayed out.
4. Touch **Set date**. The Date Adjustment window appears, as shown in **Figure 3**.
5. Touch the day on the calendar to which you wish to set the date. Touch the calendar and move your finger up or down to go to the next or previous month, respectively. The date is set.
6. Touch **Set time**. The Time Adjustment window appears, as shown in **Figure 4**.
7. Touch the hour and minute and slide your finger up or down. The time is set.

To set the time zone, touch **Select time zone** on the Date & Time Settings screen. A list of available time zones appears, as shown in **Figure 5**. Touch a time zone in the list. The time zone is set.

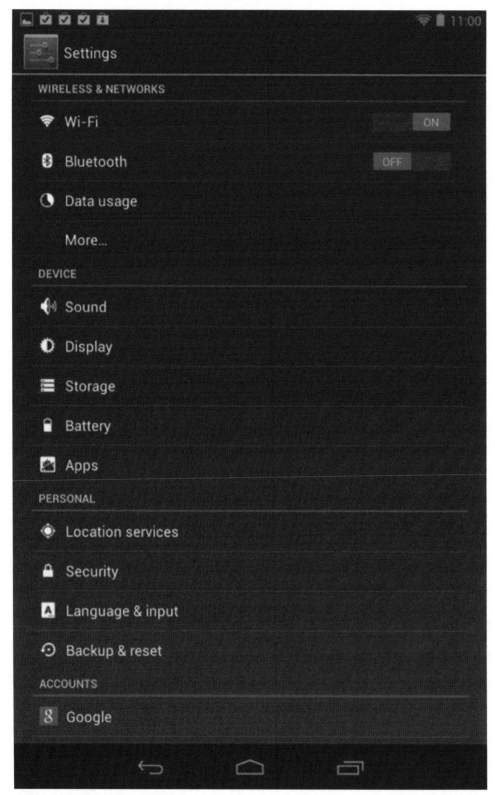

Figure 1: Settings Screen

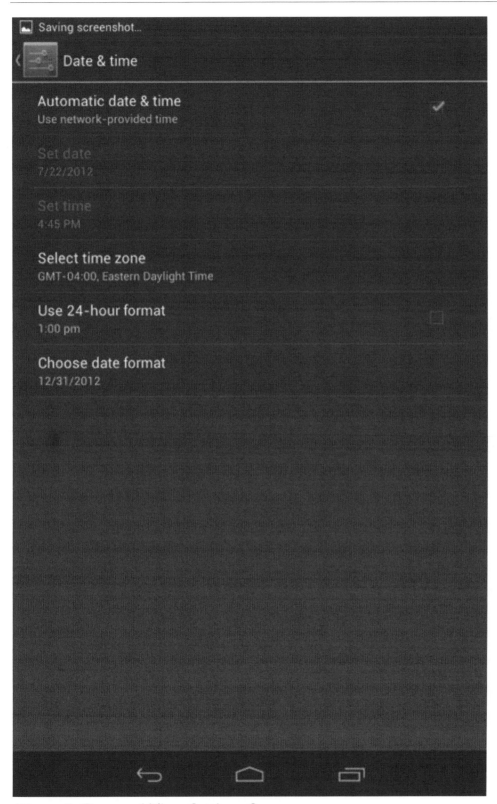

Figure 2: Date and Time Settings Screen

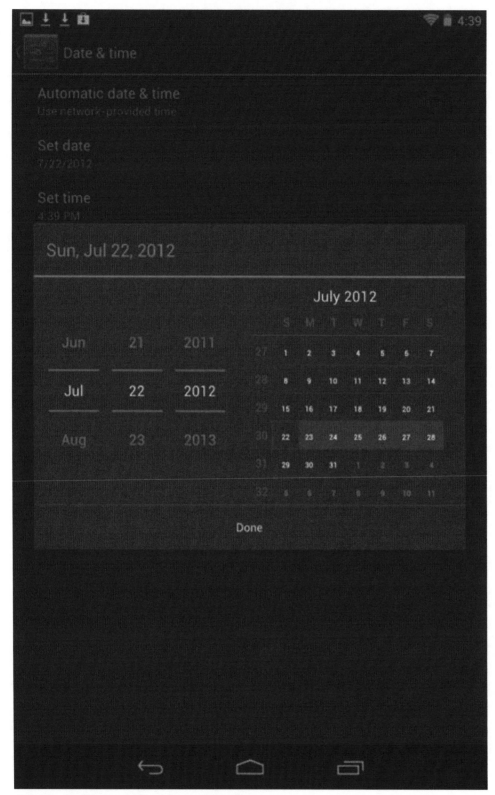

Figure 3: Date Adjustment Window

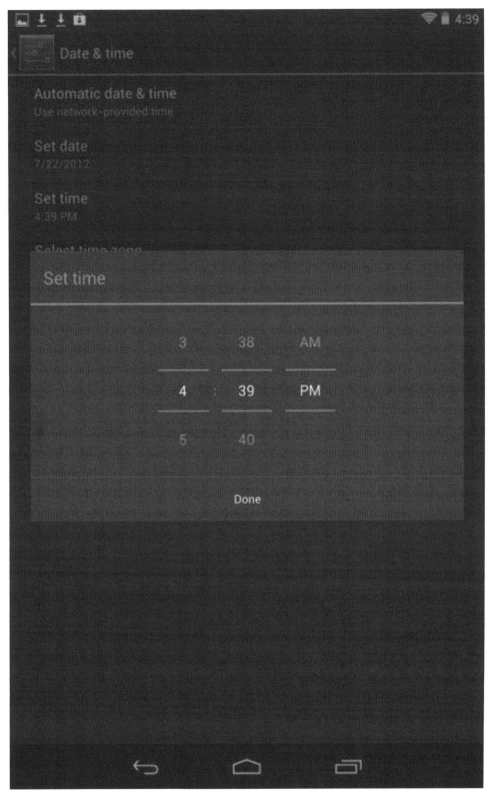

Figure 4: Time Adjustment Window

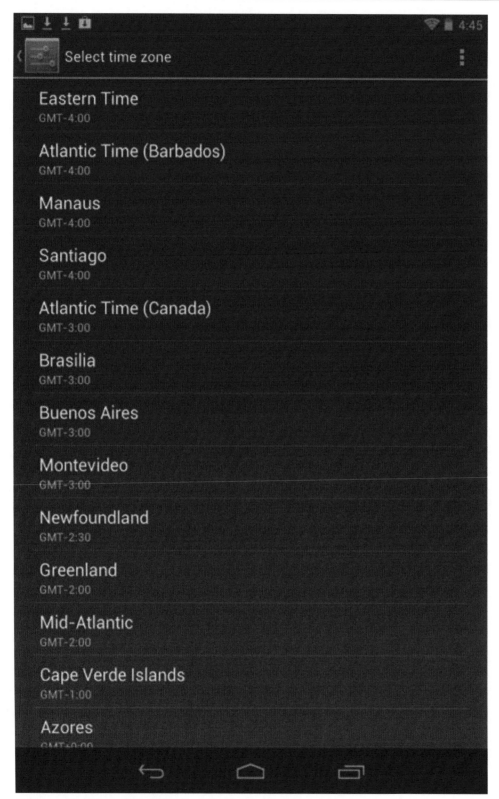

Figure 5: List of Available Time Zones

2. Turning 24-hour Format On or Off

Displaying the time in military, or 24-hour, format may be more convenient for those used to international time formats. To turn on 24-hour format:

1. Touch the icon on the Home screen, or touch the ⊞ icon and then touch the icon. The Settings screen appears.
2. Touch **Date & time**. The Date and Time Settings screen appears.
3. Touch **Use 24-hour format**. A ✓ mark appears next to 'Use 24-hour format' and the feature is turned on.
4. Touch **Use 24-hour format** again. The ✓ mark disappears and the feature is turned off.

3. Selecting the Date Format

The date can be displayed in several different formats. Some formats, like dd/mm/yyyy or yyyy/mm/dd may be more convenient than others for non-American users. To select the Date format:

1. Touch the icon on the Home screen, or touch the ⊞ icon and then touch the icon. The Settings screen appears.
2. Touch **Date & time**. The Date and Time Settings screen appears.
3. Touch **Choose date format**. A list of available Date formats appears, as shown in **Figure 6**.
4. Touch the desired format. The format is selected and will be used to display the date.

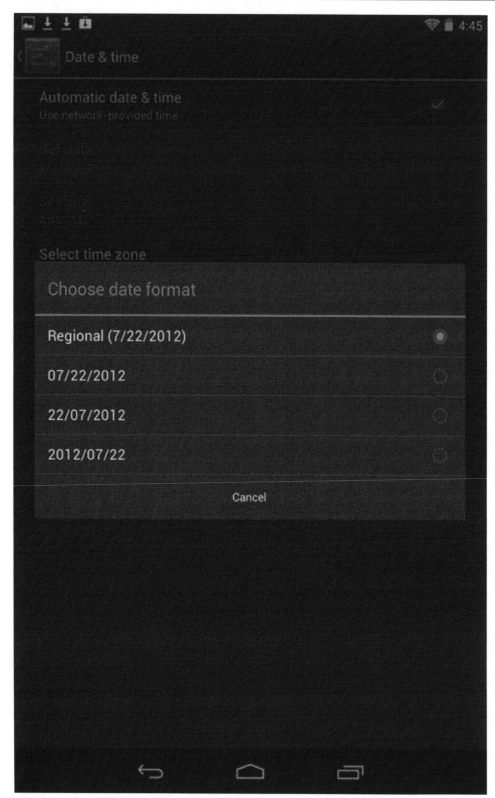

Figure 6: List of Available Date Formats

Tips and Tricks

Table of Contents

1. Maximizing Battery Life

There are several things that you can do to increase the battery life of the Nexus 7:

- Lock the Nexus 7 whenever it is not in use. To lock the device, press the **Power/Sleep** button once.

- Keep the Sleep Timer set to a small amount of time before it dims and turns off the screen when the Nexus 7 is idle. Refer to *"Setting the Amount of Time Before the Device Locks Itself"* on page 255 to learn how to change the Sleep Timer.

- Turn down the brightness or turn on Automatic Brightness. Refer to *"Adjusting the Brightness"* on page 247 to learn how to change Brightness settings.

- Turn off Wi-Fi and Bluetooth when you are not using them. Refer to *"Connecting to an Alternate Wi-Fi Network"* on page 231 to learn how to turn Wi-Fi off. Refer to *"Using Bluetooth"* on page 235 to learn how to turn off Bluetooth.

- Do not use the internet for extended periods of time. Using Wi-Fi cuts down the battery life significantly.

- Do not use the camera, if possible. The camera uses a lot of battery power.

- Close applications that are running in the background. Refer to *"Closing Applications Running in the Background"* on page 49 to learn how.

2. Checking the Amount of Available Memory

To check the amount of available memory at any time, touch the icon on the Home screen, or touch the icon and then touch the icon. The Settings screen appears. Touch **Storage**. The available memory appears under 'Available'.

3. Freeing Up Memory

There are two actions that can free up memory on the Nexus 7: uninstalling applications and removing temporary internet files stored by the Chrome browser. Refer to *"Quickly Uninstalling Applications"* below to learn how to uninstall an application. Refer to *"Clearing the Data that is Used to Speed Up Browsing"* on page 170 to learn how to delete temporary internet files stored by Chrome.

4. Viewing the Full Horizontal Keyboard

The full horizontal keyboard provides much better accuracy when typing than the vertical keyboard. Simply rotate the Nexus 7 horizontally while typing to turn on the horizontal keyboard in applications that support it. Refer to *"Screen or keyboard does not rotate"* on page 312 if you are having trouble.

5. Quickly Uninstalling Applications

Getting rid of applications you no longer use will reduce clutter and free up memory. While applications may be uninstalled from Settings, this is a rather long process. To quickly uninstall an application:

1. Touch the ⊞ icon at the bottom of the Home screen. The Applications screen appears.
2. Touch and hold an application icon. The Home screen appears and 'Uninstall' appears at the top of the screen.
3. Drag the application icon over the word 'Uninstall'. A confirmation window appears.
4. Touch **OK**. The application is uninstalled.

6. Turning the Automatic Addition of Widgets On or Off

By default, every time you purchase an application in the Play Store, the widget for that application is added to your Home screen (if one is available). To prevent widgets from automatically appearing on the Home screen:

1. Touch the ![icon] icon on the Home screen, or touch the ![icon] icon and then touch the ![icon] icon. The Play Store opens.
2. Touch **My Apps** in the upper right-hand corner of the screen. The Downloads screen appears.
3. Touch the ![icon] icon in the upper right-hand corner of the screen. The Market menu appears.
4. Touch **Settings**. The Market Settings screen appears.
5. Touch **Auto-add widgets**. The ![checkmark] mark disappears and widgets will no longer be added automatically.
6. Touch **Auto-add widgets** again if you want to turn the feature back on. The ![checkmark] mark appears and widgets will be added automatically.

7. Viewing the Desktop Version of a Website

By default, the Chrome browser displays mobile versions of websites. You can also view the desktop version of a website, if it is available. To view the desktop version of a website:

1. Touch the ![icon] icon on the Home screen, or touch the ![icon] icon and then touch the ![icon] icon. The Chrome browser opens.
2. Navigate to a website. Refer to *"Navigating to a Website"* on page 138 to learn how.
3. Touch the ![icon] icon in the upper right-hand corner of the screen. The Chrome menu appears.
4. Touch **Request desktop site**. The desktop version of the website appears, if one is available.

8. Accessing the Settings Screen Quickly

Instead of navigating through the list of applications to find the ▨ icon, you can access the Settings screen by touching the status bar at the top of the screen (which contains the time and

battery level) and sliding your finger down to open the Notifications Center. Then, touch the ▨ icon. The Settings screen appears.

9. Taking Pictures and Capturing Video

Although the Nexus 7 has a 1.2 megapixel front-facing camera, it does not come with a camera application. You can download a third-party application at **https://play.google.com/store/apps/details?id=com.modaco.cameralauncher**. Once installed, you can take pictures and capture video. In order to capture video, touch the ▨ icon in the Camera application to switch to the camcorder.

10. Deleting Pictures and Videos Quickly

Warning: When using the following method of deleting pictures and videos, no confirmation dialog will appear. Once deleted, pictures and videos cannot be restored. Make sure that you do not want the picture or video before deleting it.

There are several ways to delete pictures and videos from the Gallery. Refer to *"Deleting Pictures"* on page 70 to learn about one of these methods. To delete a picture or video quickly:

1. Open the picture or video in Full-Screen mode. Refer to *"Browsing Pictures"* on page 54 to learn how.
2. Touch a picture or video with two fingers spread apart and bring them close together. A film strip of pictures and videos appears.
3. Touch a picture or video and slide it up or down until it fades out. The picture or video is deleted.

11. Clearing the Data Stored by a Single Website

If you do not wish to delete all data stored by every website that you have visited, you can instead delete the data stored by a single website. Refer to *"Clearing the Data that is Used to Speed Up Browsing"* on page 170 to learn how to delete all website data. To clear the data stored by an individual website:

1. Touch the ⬡ icon on the Home screen, or touch the ⊞ icon and then touch the ⬡ icon. The Chrome browser opens.
2. Touch the ⋮ icon in the upper right-hand corner of the browser. The Chrome menu appears.
3. Touch **Settings**. The Chrome Settings screen appears.
4. Touch **Content settings**. The Content Settings screen appears.
5. Touch **Website settings**. A list of previously visited websites appears.
6. Touch the name of a website. The Website Settings screen appears.
7. Touch **Clear stored data**. A confirmation dialog appears.
8. Touch **Clear all**. The data stored by the selected website is deleted.

12. Taking Away a Website's Access to Your Location

Some websites will be able to access your location, if you allow them to do so. To take away a website's access to your location:

1. Touch the ⬡ icon on the Home screen, or touch the ⊞ icon and then touch the ⬡ icon. The Chrome browser opens.
2. Touch the ⋮ icon in the upper right-hand corner of the browser. The Chrome menu appears.
3. Touch **Settings**. The Chrome Settings screen appears.
4. Touch **Content settings**. The Content Settings screen appears.
5. Touch **Website settings**. A list of previously visited websites appears. The websites that have access to your location have the ◎ icon next to them.
6. Touch a website that can access your location. The Website Settings screen appears.
7. Touch **Location access**. The ☑ mark disappears and the website no longer has access to your location. Repeat steps 6 and 7 for all websites with access to your location.

13. Zooming in on a Link in the Chrome Browser

Websites with a large amount of content may be easier to view when you are zoomed out. However, it is difficult to see links when doing so. To zoom in on a group of links in the Chrome browser, touch and hold a single link. A magnifying glass appears and the links surrounding the one that you touched become visible (as well as the one that you touched). Touch one of the links to follow it.

14. Clearing One or All Notifications

You may clear all notifications at once in the Notification center. To do so, touch the status bar at the top of the screen (containing the clock and battery level) and drag down. The Notifications center appears. Touch the icon. All notifications are cleared. You may also clear a single notification by touching it and sliding your finger to the left or right. The notification is cleared.

15. Using Voice Search in Google Now

Google Now is a handy search assistant introduced in Android 4.1 Jelly Bean, which responds to voice commands. To activate Google Now, touch and hold the ⬠ key and slide your finger up to **Google**. Google Now opens. Touch the 🎤 icon to activate the Voice Search. Alternatively, you may say "Google" if Hotword Detection is turned on. Refer to *"Customizing Voice Search Settings"* on page 283 to learn how to turn it on. You can say one of the phrases below followed by your query when using Google Now:

- Map of…

- Directions to…

- Navigate to…

- Go to…

- Send email…

- Note to self…

- Set alarm…

- Listen to…

16. Turning Google Now On or Off

You may turn off Google Now altogether. To turn Google Now on or off:

1. Touch and hold the ⬠ key and slide your finger up to **Google**. Google Now opens.
2. Touch the ▮ icon in the lower right-hand corner of the screen. The Google Now menu appears.
3. Touch **Settings**. The Google Now Settings screen appears.
4. Touch **Google Now**. The Google Now screen appears.
5. Touch the [ON] switch in the upper right-hand corner of the screen. The [OFF] switch appears and a confirmation dialog appears. Touch **Also turn off Location History** if you want to turn off the Location History.
6. Touch **Turn off**. Google Now is turned off.
7. Repeat steps 1-3 and then touch **Yes, I'm in**. Google Now turns on.

17. Viewing the Home Screens in Landscape View

By default, the Nexus 7 does not allow you to rotate the Home screen in order to view it in Landscape view. However, the Nova Launcher application, which can be found at **https://play.google.com/store/apps/details?id=com.teslacoilsw.launcher**, will allow you to do so. Once the application is downloaded, enable Home screen rotation by doing the following:

1. Touch the 🔧 icon, or touch the ⦂⦂⦂ icon and then touch the 🔧 icon. The Nova Launcher Settings screen appears.
2. Touch **Look and feel**. The Look and Feel Settings screen appears.
3. Touch **Screen orientation**. The Screen Orientation options appear.
4. Touch **Auto-rotate**. The Home screens will now rotate when you rotate the device. When viewing a Home screen in Landscape view, the Application dock will appear on the right side of the screen.

18. Controlling Wireless Settings and Brightness from the Home Screen

Instead of navigating to the Settings screen to adjust Wireless and Brightness settings, use the Power Control widget, which comes pre-installed on the Nexus 7. To add the Power Control widget to the Home screen:

1. Touch the  icon. A list of all installed applications and widgets appears.
2. Scroll to the right and touch and hold the 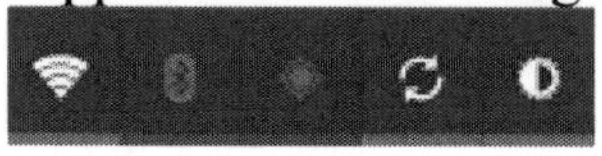 icon. The Home screen appears.
3. Drag the widget to an empty space and release the screen. The Power Control widget is added to the Home screen.
4. Touch an icon on the widget to turn the corresponding feature on or off. The Power Control widget offers the following toggle switches:

- Wi-Fi
- Bluetooth
- GPS
- Data Syncing
- Brightness

19. Adding a Navigation Shortcut to the Home Screen

Instead of opening the Maps application every time you wish to navigate to an address that you often visit, add a Navigation shortcut to the Home screen. To add a Navigation shortcut:

1. Touch the [icon] icon. A list of all installed applications and widgets appears.

2. Scroll to the right and touch and hold the [icon] icon. The Home screen appears.
3. Drag the Navigation shortcut to an empty space and release the screen. The Navigation shortcut is added to the Home screen and the Destination screen appears.
4. Enter the address and touch **Save**. The Navigation shortcut is set up. Touch the shortcut at any time to navigate to the selected address.

20. Capturing a Screenshot

To capture what is on the screen and save it as a photo, press and hold the **Volume Down** and **Power/Sleep** buttons simultaneously. Release the buttons and your screen will momentarily flash a white color. The screenshot is stored in the 'Screenshot' album.

Troubleshooting

Table of Contents

1. Nexus 7 does not turn on

Try one of the following:

- Recharge the battery using the included wall charger. If the battery power is extremely low, the screen will not turn on for several minutes. Do NOT use the USB port on your computer to charge the Nexus 7; it may not properly charge the device.

- Replace the battery. If you purchased the Nexus 7 a long time ago and have charged and discharged the battery approximately 300-400 times, you may need to replace the battery. In this case, the device may still turn on, but the battery will die much faster than in a newer device.

- Press and hold the **Power/Sleep** button for 30 seconds. The device should reset and turn on.

2. Nexus 7 is not responding

If the Nexus 7 is frozen or is not responding, try one or more of the following. These steps solve most problems on the Nexus 7:

- **Restart the Nexus 7** - If the Nexus 7 freezes while running an application, hold down the Volume Up button on and the Power/Sleep button . The Nexus 7 restarts.

- **Remove Media** - Some downloaded applications or music may freeze up the Nexus 7. Try deleting some of the media after restarting the Nexus 7. Refer to *"Uninstalling an Application"* on page 43 or *"Quickly Uninstalling Applications"* on page 301 to learn how to delete an application.

- **Reset the Tablet** - If the above suggestions do not help, you may also reset and erase all data at once by doing the following:

Warning: Any erased data is not recoverable.

1. Touch the ![icon] icon on the Home screen, or touch the ![icon] icon and then touch the ![icon] icon. The Settings screen appears
2. Touch **Backup & reset**. The Backup & Reset screen appears.
3. Touch **Factory data reset**. The Factory Reset screen appears.
4. Touch **Reset tablet** at the bottom of the screen. The Nexus 7 is reset and all data is erased.

3. Can't surf the web

Make sure that Wi-Fi is turned on and the Nexus 7 is connected to a network. If you performed all of the steps in *"Performing First-Time Setup"* on page 16, then you are already connected. Refer to *"Connecting to an Alternate Wi-Fi Network"* on page 231 to learn how to connect to a different network.

4. Screen or keyboard does not rotate

If the screen does not rotate, or the full horizontal keyboard is not appearing when rotating the Nexus 7, it may be one of the following issues:

- The application does not support the horizontal view.

- The Nexus 7 is lying flat when rotating. Hold the device upright for the view to change in applications that support it.

- You are viewing one of the Home screens. By default, the screen will not rotate when you are viewing a Home screen. Refer to *"Viewing the Home Screens in Landscape View"* on page 307 to learn how to use a third-party application to rotate the Home screens.

5. Application does not download or install correctly

Sometimes applications may not download or install correctly. If this happens, try uninstalling and re-installing the application. Refer to *"Uninstalling an Application"* on page 43 and *"Purchasing Applications"* on page 38 to learn how.

6. Touchscreen does not respond as expected

If the touchscreen does not perform the desired functions or does not work at all, try the following:

- Remove the screen protector, if you use one.

- Make sure that your hands are clean and dry and that the touchscreen is clean. Oily fingers can make the screen dirty and unresponsive.

- Restart the Nexus 7.

- Make sure that the touchscreen does not come in contact with anything but skin. Scratches on the screen are permanent and may cause the device to malfunction.

7. Device is hot to the touch

When running some applications for extended periods of time, the Nexus 7 may become hot. This is normal and will not harm the device in any way.

8. Computer does not recognize the Nexus 7

If your computer does not recognize the Nexus 7, try one of the following:

- Only use the provided USB cable to connect the Nexus 7 to your computer.

- Connect the device directly to the computer, since some USB hubs will not work.

- Make sure that the correct drivers are installed on your computer, if any are needed. If using a Mac, make sure that you have installed the Android File Transfer application. Download this application at **www.android.com/filetransfer**. Without this application, the Nexus 7 will not be recognized by your Mac.

9. Photo or video does not display

If the Nexus 7 cannot open a photo or video, the file type is most likely not supported. Supported file types include:

Images

- BMP
- GIF
- JPG
- PNG
- WEBP

Videos

- MPEG4
- VP8
- AVC

10. Tablet does not detect a Bluetooth device

If the Nexus 7 does not detect a Bluetooth device, try one of the following:

- Move the Nexus 7 closer to the Bluetooth device
- Make sure Bluetooth is enabled on the Nexus 7
- Make sure Bluetooth is enabled on the Bluetooth device.

11. What to do if you could not solve your problem

Contact Google Play Help at 855-836-3987 or check the Google Play Help Center at **http://support.google.com/googleplay/?hl=en**.

Index

Google Nexus 7 Survival Guide

from MobileReference

Author: Toly K
Editor: Julia Rouhart

This book is also available in electronic format from the following vendors:

- **Barnesandnoble.com**
- **iBooks for iPhone and iPad**

MobileReference is a brand of SoundTells, LLC.
Please email questions and comments to support@soundtells.com. Normally we are able to respond to your email on the same business day.

MobileReference®. Intelligence in Your Pocket™.

About MobileReference

MobileReference is a Boston-based publisher of eBooks and reference materials. Since 2003, MobileReference has published over 10,000 Fiction Books, Travel Guides, Phrasebooks, History and Philosophy eBooks, Study Guides, Medical and Health Reference eBooks, Encyclopedias, and Dictionaries. MobileReference eBooks are designed for optimal navigation on mobile devices including smartphones, tablet PC's and eReaders like the Amazon Kindle, B&N Nook, and Sony Reader. MobileReference eBooks are available at major distributors including Google Books, Apple iBooks, B&N Nook store, Sony Reader Store, Kobo, and more.

Trademarks:

Nexus 7 is a trademark of Google Inc. Mac is a trademark of Apple Inc. Kindle is a trademark of Amazon.com Inc. Nova Launcher is a trademark of TeslaCoil Software. All other trademarks are the property of their respective owners.

Other Books from the Author of the Survival Guide Series, Toly K

Guides for Tablets

iPad Survival Guide
iPad 2 Survival Guide
Motorola Xoom Survival Guide
Galaxy Tab Survival Guide
Nook Tablet Survival Guide
Kindle Fire Survival Guide

Guides for eReaders

Kindle Touch Survival Guide
Kindle Survival Guide
Kindle 2011 Survival Guide
Nook Survival Guide
Nook Color Survival Guide
Nook Simple Touch Survival Guide
Nook Simple Touch GlowLight Survival Guide
Nook Tablet Survival Guide
Kobo Survival Guide
Kobo Touch Survival Guide
Sony Reader Survival Guide

Guides for Smartphones

iPhone 4 and 4S Survival Guide
iPhone 3G and 3GS Survival Guide
HTC Incredible Survival Guide
Samsung Droid Fascinate Survival Guide
Galaxy Note Survival Guide
HTC Droid 4G Survival Guide
Galaxy Nexus Survival Guide
Droid X Survival Guide
Motorola Atrix Survival Guide
HTC Vivid Survival Guide

Other Guides

iPod Touch Survival Guide
iTunes for PC Survival Guide
Switching from PC to Mac Survival Guide
How to find and Download Free eBooks
iPad Apps for Scientists Survival Guide
iPad Games for Kids Survival Guide
Pages Survival Guide
Keynote Survival Guide
Numbers Survival Guide